IPOLAR SORDER

The Essential Guide

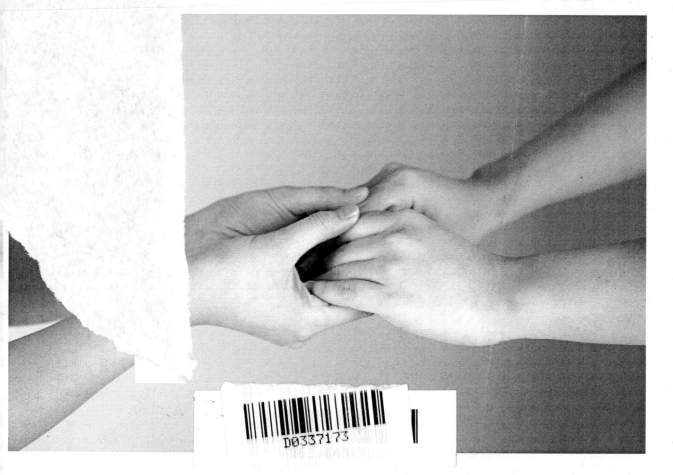

First published in Great Britain in 2011 by
Need2Know
Remus House
Coltsfoot Drive
Peterborough
PE2 9BF
Telephone 01733 898103
Fax 01733 313524
www.need2knowbooks.co.uk

Contents

Introduction

Bipolar disorder, formerly called manic depression, is a common condition affecting around one in 100 adults at some point in their life. Worldwide, it affects about 254 million people, with 12m in the US and 2.4m in the UK.

Bipolar usually starts when you're a teenager, or shortly afterwards and – unlike 'unipolar' depression, which is more common in women – affects both sexes equally. As its older name suggests, it is characterised by severe mood swings that usually last several weeks or even months.

The exact nature of someone's illness will be unique to them, but these moods typically swing between low or 'depressive', with feelings of intense unhappiness and despair; and high or 'manic', with feelings of supreme confidence, euphoria and boundless energy. People with bipolar disorder may also experience a 'mixed state', perhaps being in a depressed mood but with the restlessness and hyperactivity of a manic episode.

Having bipolar disorder can be a frightening, bewildering experience, especially before you get treatment. You may find yourself swinging from dark, unhappy moods to periods where you barely eat or sleep, and your friends and family will probably be concerned about your welfare. You may even experience strange, distorted thinking and hallucinations. When you don't understand why this is happening to you, it's easy to feel isolated, worried and confused.

The good news is that treatment of bipolar disorder has made huge advances in the last few decades. If you are diagnosed with bipolar, you are likely to be treated with a combination of drugs, which will include a mood stabiliser like lithium, an antidepressant to combat the lows, and perhaps other drugs. Your psychiatrist may also recommend talking therapy, like cognitive behavioural therapy (CBT) or counselling.

Another vital aspect of managing bipolar disorder is 'self-care', in which you learn to recognise the things that trigger your low and high moods, to look after yourself in terms of exercise, diet, sleep and the amount of stress you're under at any given time. Learning to take good care of yourself is a powerful tool for managing your own wellbeing.

This book will help you understand whether you might have bipolar disorder and, if so, the kind of help that is available to you and the people closest to you. It will explain what happens when you receive a diagnosis – and why it's crucial that this is made as early as possible. As you read on you will discover which mental health professionals will help and support you, and the best options for treatment, both privately and on the NHS.

You will also learn what causes bipolar disorder; its symptoms and the effect it can have on your life; the way it's usually treated; how you can help yourself; and what your friends, family or partner need to know – they are likely to need help and support too.

The most important thing to remember is that many people with bipolar disorder lead happy, fulfilling lives as long as they receive the correct treatment and look after themselves properly. And the first step on your journey to a healthier, happier life is to read this book.

Finally, a word of thanks to all the people who were brave and honest enough to describe their own experience of living with bipolar disorder. Despite the difficulties they describe, they are testament to the fact that, with the right treatment and support, people with bipolar can lead a rich, fulfilling life.

Disclaimer

This book is only for general information about bipolar disorder and is not intended to replace medical advice, although it can be used alongside it. Anyone who suspects they may have bipolar disorder should contact their GP in the first instance.

Names of some case studies have been changed.

Chapter One

What is Bipolar Disorder?

We all have mood swings, days when we feel happy and excited and others when nothing seems to cheer us up. Being moody is perfectly natural and part of the human condition. But for some people, those mood swings can be far more severe. They lurch from periods of extreme happiness, energy and supreme self-confidence to times when they are exhausted, low and miserable, lacking any self-belief or confidence that things will ever look brighter.

For a long time, if you suffered from these mood swings, psychiatrists would have said you had manic depression. But in 1980 the American Psychiatric Association (APA) renamed this condition bipolar disorder, to reflect what the APA called its 'bi-polarity', or dual nature (bipolar actually means 'both poles'). Some people, including well-known bipolar sufferer Stephen Fry, prefer the old name, because they feel it describes the illness, with its swings from being manic to feeling depressed, more accurately. Still, others think 'multi-polar disorder' is a better term, because there's much more to the illness than just going up or down.

Although, of course, we need to call it something, perhaps using labels to describe people and their unique personality, life experiences, physical and mental health challenges is unhelpful. It's also important to note that everyone's experience of bipolar disorder is different. Some experts call it a 'spectrum disorder', because symptoms can range from very mild at one end of the spectrum to severe at the other.

'Bipolar disorder is a serious mental health problem involving extreme swings of mood (highs and lows).'

MDF: the BiPolar Organisation.

What is a mood disorder?

A mood disorder is the term given for a group of diagnoses in the *Diagnostic and Statistical Manual of Mental Disorders* (also called DSM-IV, the manual psychiatrists and other mental health professionals use to diagnose mental illness) where a disturbance in the person's mood is the main underlying feature. Mood disorders include dysthymia (chronic minor depression), major depressive disorder (unipolar depression) and manic-depressive disorder (bipolar disorder).

Unlike the first two conditions, as we have seen bipolar disorder is characterised by a swing between different moods. According to Jan Scott, in her book *Overcoming Mood Swings: A Self-Help Guide Using Cognitive Behavioral Techniques* (see book list), problematic mood swings – as opposed to normal changes in mood – share some or all of these characteristics. They are often:

- Unpredictable – frequently fluctuating but without obvious reasons.

- Uncontrollable – emotional responses that seem inappropriate reactions to events and are beyond your control.

- Extreme – with moods always experienced as intense highs or lows.

- Excessive – with frequent ups and downs occurring over many years.

- Extensive – marked changes of mood that last a long time.

- Accompanied by associated changes – in your thoughts, the way you behave, and possibly in the biological systems that impact on day-to-day functioning.

- Disruptive to lives – causing significant problems for the individual experiencing them and/or for others.

Bipolar disorder shares some elements with, but is different from, a number of other conditions. In generalised anxiety disorder (GAD), sufferers worry almost constantly and excessively about problems that most people think are minor, or events that are unlikely to occur. GAD affects about 3-4% of the population at any one time in the US and most other Western countries, and women are twice as likely to be affected as men. GAD is also associated with panic attacks – sudden, unexpected episodes of intense fear or terror, often accompanied by shortness of breath, rapid heartbeat and choking sensations.

Stress is something that affects us all, at some time, but chronic stress often affects those working long hours or under a great deal of pressure. If left untreated, stress can cause a range of physical and mental problems, such as high blood pressure, ulcers, anxiety, depression, burnout and breakdown.

Post-traumatic stress disorder (PTSD) is caused by a deeply disturbing experience or prolonged series of these experiences. PTSD is often associated with servicemen and women who have undergone the trauma of war, but it can affect anyone who has been involved in or witnessed traumatic events. It may well cause flashbacks, when the traumatic event is re-experienced through memories, nightmares or hallucinations.

Types of bipolar disorder

We will explore these ideas in greater detail throughout the book, but for now let's look at the two main types of bipolar disorder, as described in the DSM-IV:

Bipolar I

To be diagnosed with Bipolar I, you will have had at least one manic episode throughout your lifetime, which will have lasted for longer than one week. Some people with Bipolar I will only have manic episodes, but most will also have periods of depression. Around one percent of the population is thought to develop this type of bipolar disorder at some point in their lives.

Bipolar II

If you are diagnosed with Bipolar II, you will have experienced more than one episode of severe depression, but only mild manic episodes, known as 'hypomania'. Between four and five percent of the population is thought to have experienced Bipolar II at some point.

The diagram on the following page, originally printed in Jan Scott's *Overcoming Mood Swings*, makes clear how Bipolar I and II differ, as well as the difference between them and purely depressive mood disorders.

Pattern of mood changes in mood disorders

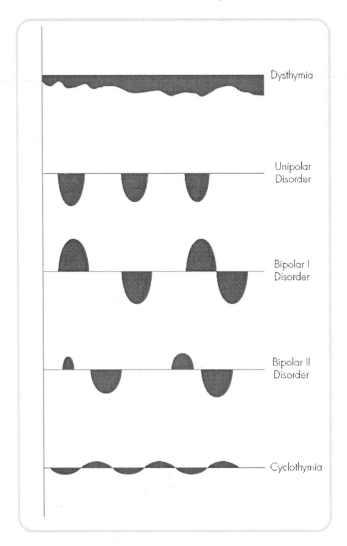

Table from *Overcoming Mood Swings* by Jan Scott (Constable & Robinson, London, 2000) by kind permission of the publishers.

Need2Know

Rapid cycling

This is when you have more than four mood swings in a 12-month period. Rapid cycling affects around one in 10 people with bipolar disorder and can happen with both types.

Cyclothymia

If a person has depressive and manic symptoms lasting for at least two years, but they are not severe enough to qualify as bipolar disorder (those symptoms are not 'full-blown'), they may be diagnosed with cyclothymia, which is a milder form of bipolar disorder. Cyclothymia is often characterised by frequent short periods of hypomania and depressive symptoms, with periods of stability inbetween. There is evidence that some people with cyclothymia will experience more and more severe mood swings until they eventually develop either Bipolar I or II.

It's worth mentioning that cyclothymia is tricky to diagnose – how do you distinguish between someone who is moody or emotional and someone who is mildly bipolar? Even mental health experts argue about this, because the definition of what's 'normal' varies widely between cultures and in different settings. For example, what's considered flamboyant behaviour by an artist may be viewed with suspicion in a corporate setting. The same goes for Mediterranean and Northern European cultures, which have very different attitudes to expressing or withholding your emotions. What seems perfectly normal to Italians may be viewed as odd, even unhealthy by the famously stiff upper-lipped British.

Symptoms of depression and mania

Bipolar disorder is characterised by mood swings between two states: lows, known as depression, and highs, known as mania. The length of time you might spend in each state is extremely variable – it can be days, weeks or months. Some people even experience rapid mood swings throughout the course of a single day.

Again, the exact nature of your symptoms will be unique to you, but here's a guide to some of the most commonly experienced symptoms in both states.

Depression

It's important to distinguish between feeling a little bit fed up or down in the dumps, as we all do from time to time, and clinical depression, which can feel a great deal worse and usually lasts a lot longer – sometimes for months on end. People experiencing this type of depression commonly experience:

- Feelings of unhappiness that won't go away.
- Feeling that you want to burst into tears for no apparent reason.
- Losing interest in things and being unable to enjoy them.
- Feeling restless, agitated and irritable.
- Losing self-confidence.
- Feeling useless, inadequate and hopeless.
- Negative thinking and thoughts of suicide.
- Finding it hard to concentrate or make decisions.
- Losing appetite and weight.
- Difficulty getting to sleep and waking earlier than usual.
- Feeling exhausted.
- Loss of libido.
- Feeling isolated and avoiding contact with others.

Mania

Again, what psychiatrists call 'mania' is more severe than being a bit hyperactive or excitable, especially as the mania escalates. If you are experiencing a manic episode for the first time, you may not realise that anything's wrong – although your family, friends and colleagues will. This is how mania commonly affects people:

- Feeling very happy and excited.
- Getting irritated with others who don't share your optimistic outlook.

- Feeling more important than usual.
- Bursting with new and exciting ideas.
- Moving quickly from one idea to another.
- Being full of energy.
- Being unable or unwilling to sleep.
- Having an increased interest in sex.
- Making grandiose and unrealistic plans.
- Being very active and moving around quickly.
- Behaving strangely.
- Talking very quickly – so that others find it hard to understand you.
- Making odd, impulsive decisions, sometimes with disastrous consequences.
- Spending recklessly.
- Being over-familiar with or hyper-critical of others.
- Being generally less inhibited.

Mixed state

Some people with bipolar disorder experience symptoms of both extremes at the same time, for example a depressed mood with the restlessness and overactivity of a manic episode.

Psychotic symptoms

If an episode of mania or depression becomes very severe, you may experience 'psychotic' symptoms.

- In a manic episode – these will tend to be grandiose beliefs about yourself. You may think you are on an important mission to save the planet, for example, or to bring about world peace. You may also believe you have special powers or abilities.

- In a depressive episode – you may feel you are uniquely guilty, that you are worse than everyone else, or even that you don't exist.

You may also experience hallucinations, when you hear, smell, feel or see things that aren't there.

Between episodes

It used to be thought that if you had bipolar disorder, you would return to normal inbetween mood swings. Mental health experts now know this is not true for many people with bipolar disorder. For example, you may experience mild depressive symptoms and 'distorted thinking' even when you seem to be better. Again, the ways in which you might cycle between highs and lows, and what you experience inbetween those cycles, will be unique to you.

Who gets bipolar disorder?

Unlike 'unipolar' depression (where you only experience periods of low mood without the highs), which is thought to affect more women than men, bipolar disorder affects men and women in equal numbers. There is some evidence that between the ages of 16 and 25, bipolar disorder affects more men than women. Over the age of 26, more women seem to be affected. It's also thought that women are more likely to experience rapid cycling, in which moods change very quickly, and mixed states, where symptoms of both extremes are felt at the same time.

The average age of people being diagnosed with bipolar disorder is 19. This has dropped from 32 during the mid-1990s, probably because there's an increased awareness of the illness and drug abuse has increased (one of the lifestyle factors that can trigger bipolar disorder and make symptoms more severe).

We also experience a very different range of stressors now, and there has been a huge increase in the number of children diagnosed with bipolar disorder in the US, which has brought the average age down. This is a highly controversial area – many psychiatrists, especially in the UK, are reluctant to diagnose children with bipolar disorder, and even more reluctant to prescribe

14

them the kind of powerful medication routinely taken by American kids. (In the US, the number of children diagnosed with bipolar disorder has increased fivefold in the last eight years and children as young as two or three are being diagnosed.)

Many experts, even if they don't believe that young children can have bipolar disorder, do think they can behave in ways that predict bipolar disorder in later life. If so, this would allow doctors and parents to carefully monitor at-risk children's lifestyles and ensure they don't develop bipolar disorder when they are older – we'll look in more detail at the importance of your lifestyle in chapter 9.

It is possible for bipolar disorder to be diagnosed in the elderly, but this is fairly unusual and the symptoms are different – older people tend to have shorter, more severe cycles. And most people diagnosed over the age of 50 will have a history of either depression or mania.

Co-existing illnesses and conditions

It's very common for people with bipolar to engage in substance abuse (misusing alcohol and/or recreational drugs), but the reasons for this link are not clear. Some people with bipolar disorder may try to treat or mask their symptoms with alcohol or drugs – self-medicating to make themselves feel better in the short term. During a manic episode, the difficulty in self-control may lead to someone drinking too much or taking illegal drugs. But substance abuse may trigger or prolong bipolar symptoms – alcohol is a depressant and many recreational drugs, like cocaine and ecstasy, cause severe low mood during the 'comedown'.

Anxiety disorders, such as post-traumatic stress disorder (PTSD) and social phobia (when you're extremely nervous in social situations), also co-occur among people with bipolar disorder. And bipolar co-occurs with attention deficit hyperactivity disorder (ADHD), which has some overlapping symptoms, such as restlessness and being easily distracted.

People with bipolar disorder are also at higher risk for thyroid disease, migraines, heart disease, diabetes, obesity and other physical illnesses. It's very important for people with bipolar disorder to monitor their physical and mental health and take good care of themselves – see chapter 8 for details.

Summing Up

Bipolar disorder, which used to be called manic depression, is a common mental health condition that is usually diagnosed in the teenage years or soon after. It's characterised by swings between low moods, known as depression, and highs, called mania. The exact nature of these moods, how long they last, how frequently you swing between them and how you feel between those swings will be unique to you.

The main types of bipolar disorder are Bipolar I (more prone to mania) and Bipolar II (more prone to depression). You may also be diagnosed with cyclothymia, where the mood swings are not as severe as in 'full-blown' bipolar disorder. But this can eventually develop into type I or II.

You may also experience a mixed state, in which you have symptoms of both high and low moods at the same time. And, if an episode of either depression or mania becomes very severe, you may develop psychotic symptoms, where you experience delusional thinking or hallucinations.

Chapter Two

What Causes Bipolar Disorder?

Despite decades of research, doctors and scientists are still not sure exactly what causes bipolar disorder. But rapid advances in medical fields like genetics, neuroscience and brain-imaging mean that experts do have a much clearer picture of what happens to our brains when we develop a mental illness like bipolar. According to MDF: the BiPolar Organisation, the latest research shows that there are changes to the brain's chemistry during both manic and depressive episodes. The levels of hormones like cortisol, and neurotransmitters (chemicals that transmit signals within the brain) such as serotonin and dopamine fluctuate during both high and low states, so long-term studies are currently underway trying to find out why this happens.

Medical researchers are also analysing the junctions between the neurons (brain cells) to see if there are any significant differences between people with bipolar and those without. At the moment, though, it's a 'chicken and egg' situation: are these differences caused by or do they cause the illness? But it is clear that injuries to the brain, tumours and strokes can lead to bipolar disorder, which suggests that it has something to do with important pathways in the brain being interrupted.

'Along with genes, life experience and environmental factors are hugely important.'

Professor Nick Craddock, scientific advisor to MDF: the BiPolar Organisation.

Could a faulty body clock be to blame?

Another major area of interest at the moment is 'circadian rhythms'. This is another name for the body clock that controls our sleep-wake cycle, eating habits, body temperature and hormone secretion. Some experts believe that a body clock which is not working properly might cause the mood cycles associated with bipolar disorder. Researchers at Indiana University recently found that children with bipolar disorder were likely to have an altered RORB gene (one of the 'clock genes' that controls the function of our circadian clock). And previous studies have shown that strictly regulating a bipolar patient's sleep schedule could improve extreme mood cycles, but experts weren't sure why. The new research into this faulty gene may explain the link.

Again, work is ongoing in this area, but hopefully all these avenues of research will provide answers to what causes bipolar disorder – and, more importantly, the best ways to treat it – in the near future. In the meantime, here's what we do know.

Why your genes are so important

The fact that bipolar disorder runs in families suggests there are significant genetic factors involved. Parents with bipolar have a one in 10 chance that their children will develop the illness; if both parents have bipolar those odds increase to four in 10. Although this sounds worrying, a more positive way to look at it is that, in the first case, 90% of children don't go on to develop the illness, and even if both parents are bipolar 60% of children don't develop it themselves.

But like other mental illnesses, there does seem to be a strong genetic predisposition (the likelihood that you will develop something) with bipolar. Studies of twins provide the strongest evidence for this: when identical twins are brought up in the same environment, between 40 and 70% of twins both have bipolar disorder. But when the twins are non-identical (and therefore don't share all the same genes) there is, on average, only a 10% chance that both will have bipolar. This proves that some kind of vulnerability to the illness is inherited.

However, despite what you might have read in the papers, there is no such thing as a single 'bipolar gene'. Professor Nick Craddock, head of the Cardiff University Psychiatry Service, scientific advisor to MDF: the BiPolar Organisation and one of the UK's leading experts on bipolar, explains that it's much more complicated than that. 'Because we know that genes are an important risk factor for bipolar, we are working to identify some of the gene variants that influence risk. We have discovered that there are many genes which can influence risk and any one risk variant only has a small effect. Of course, if you have a risk variant it does make it more likely you'll develop bipolar, and if you have a lot of variants, it's clearly more likely you will develop the illness. But there are many people in the general population who have a risk variant and never develop bipolar.'

The fact that there is no single bipolar gene means there is no simple genetic test to see if you have a predisposition to the illness or not. Again, experts like Professor Craddock are doing a great deal of research into this area to improve diagnosis and treatment. Elsewhere, research by the Wellcome Trust Case Control Consortium (WTCCC), a collaboration between 24 leading human geneticists, has found new genetic variants for seven major disorders – including bipolar disorder. It looks very likely that this type of research will transform the way doctors understand and treat the illness in the course of your lifetime.

What are triggers?

A number of things are thought to act as 'triggers', both for people to develop the illness for the first time and then for either high or low moods when they have developed it. As we will see in chapter 8, when we look at the ways you can help yourself, learning about the specific things that trigger your mood swings will give you a powerful set of tools to manage your illness. For now, let's look at the main things that are known to be triggers for bipolar illness.

Your lifestyle

As with any other mental or physical illness, environmental and lifestyle factors have a huge part to play in bipolar disorder. If you do have a genetic predisposition, the kind of environment you grow up in – for example, if there is a lot of financial insecurity or anger around when you are a small child – and then the type of lifestyle you lead in your teenage and adult years may play a major part in whether you go on to develop the illness or not.

Experts also believe that a stressful event, or situation, is usually required to trigger the onset of bipolar symptoms. Examples of stressful triggers include:

▒ Physical, sexual or emotional abuse.

▒ The breakdown of a relationship.

▒ The death of a close family member or loved one.

There's clearly not much you can do about the family you grow up in, or stressful triggers like bereavement. But all the research shows that making sensible lifestyle choices reduces the chance of developing full-blown bipolar, even if you have a genetic predisposition to it. As we've seen, this is especially important if one or both of your parents have bipolar disorder.

These lifestyle choices are basically the same advice we get all the time from doctors and health experts. They include:

- Eating a balanced diet, including three meals a day, healthy snacks inbetween and plenty of fresh fruit and vegetables.

- Not smoking.

- Minimising your caffeine intake: ideally, no more than two caffeinated drinks a day (and remember that lots of fizzy drinks are very high in caffeine).

- Watching your alcohol intake, sticking to the Department of Health guideline of one or two alcoholic drinks a day.

- Not taking recreational drugs like cannabis, cocaine or Ecstasy (more on this below).

- Taking regular exercise, ideally at least 30 minutes of cardiovascular exercise like running, swimming, cycling or a brisk walk five times a week.

- Enjoying plenty of mood-lifting sunlight, preferably in beautiful natural surroundings like a park or the country.

- Minimising your daily stress levels.

- Not working excessive hours and making sure you have a good work/life balance.

- Getting plenty of sleep (ideally seven to eight hours) every night.

Professor Craddock explains that these lifestyle factors can be just as important as (and sometimes more important than) the genes we inherit. 'Along with genes, life experience and environmental factors are crucial. We know that things like stress can increase the chance someone will get ill. For some people, sleep loss or substance abuse, such as taking cocaine, can trigger the illness. Heavy alcohol use, especially bingeing, can also be an important factor.'

So is it nature or nurture?

There has long been an argument about whether mental illness is caused by 'nature' (your genes) or 'nurture' (your family dynamic and environment). Traditionally, on one side were psychiatrists and doctors, on the other sociologists and psychotherapy pioneers like Sigmund Freud and Carl Jung. These days, that debate seems a bit old-fashioned and most experts agree it's a combination of both: as we've seen, a genetic predisposition followed by a lifestyle trigger like stress or sleep deprivation.

A useful way to explain this, says Professor Craddock, is with the 'sunburn analogy'. It goes like this. We all know that people with fair, often freckly skin are more at risk of sunburn. We also know that frequent or severe sunburn leads to wrinkles and, in rare cases, skin cancer.

Also, only fair-skinned people exposed to sunlight get burned, while some, using sunscreen and staying out of extreme heat, can develop a lovely tan – and those who stay inside can avoid burning altogether. Of course, even dark-skinned people with absolutely no fair-skinned genes will get sunburned if they bask in the sun on the first hot day after a long, chilly winter.

If we think about bipolar disorder in this way, even if you have fair skin (a genetic predisposition), as long as you use plenty of sunscreen and avoid the midday heat (don't get too stressed or abuse drugs and alcohol) you can avoid getting sunburn and skin cancer (developing full-blown bipolar disorder).

Why is stress a problem?

Over many thousands of years, the human body has become uniquely adapted to survive – that's one of the reasons we're the most successful animal on the planet. When we were living on the African savannah, around 200,000 years ago, we were constantly under threat from predators like lions, and from hostile tribes trying to take over our territory. To help us deal with these threats, we developed the 'fight or flight' response (actually, it's 'fight, flight or freeze', but we're only concerned with the first two here).

So if we saw a lion come racing towards us through the long grass, our brains instantly perceived a serious threat to our existence and, in microseconds, decided whether fight or flight was the best option. At the same time, glands in our body were pumping out hormones like adrenaline and noradrenalin, which prepare the body for an emergency. Our heart started racing, so it could pump more blood to the muscles we would need to fight or flee, and our breathing became fast and shallow, to oxygenate that blood and help the muscles work more efficiently.

All sorts of other physical changes happened in seconds – our palms became sweaty, pupils dilated, immune and digestive systems shut down – as we prepared for action. Now, this was all well and good when faced with a lion. Unfortunately, exactly the same process occurs when we're faced with a 21st century threat like being yelled at by our boss, threatened with redundancy or when some bloke starts chatting up our girlfriend. And because we rarely get the chance to either fight or run, none of those chemicals sloshing about in our bloodstream get burned off. One of them in particular, cortisol, does a great deal of damage to our physical and mental health – that's why chronic stress is so bad for us, especially if it goes on for extended periods. It causes headaches, indigestion, nausea and palpitations, as well as increasing anxiety, fear, anger, frustration and depression.

So it's no surprise that stress is one of the key triggers for people with bipolar – both short-term stressors like divorce or bereavement and longer-term issues like a demanding boss or excessive working hours. If you would like to know more about the 'fight or flight' response and how stress affects the brain and body, read *Stress – The Essential Guide* (Need2Know), *Why Zebras Don't Get Ulcers: The Acclaimed Guide to Stress, Stress-Related Disease and Coping*, by Robert M Sapolsky. Or for a no-nonsense guide to managing stress, try *How to Deal With Stress*, by Stephen Palmer and Cary Cooper.

The dangers of drugs

We've all had the lectures about recreational drugs enough times to know that they can be harmful, especially taken in large amounts or on a regular basis. There's a great deal of evidence showing that drugs like cannabis (especially stronger strains like skunk), cocaine, Ecstasy, amphetamines, LSD and heroin have a profound effect on our brain chemistry and therefore our moods. As Professor Craddock explained earlier, using drugs like cocaine or bingeing on alcohol can be a trigger for bipolar illness.

People often forget that alcohol is a drug, and because it's both legal and socially acceptable, we take far more of it than all the illegal drugs combined. The World Health Organization (WHO) says it's clear that alcohol plays a contributing role in the development of depression. And substance abuse is seen in up to one half of people with bipolar disorder – with alcohol the most commonly abused substance.

It's not just recreational drugs – whether legal or illegal – that must be handled with care. Treatment with antidepressants is known to cause hypomania and mania in up to a third of bipolar patients. Older tricyclic antidepressants, like amitriptyline, are especially likely to cause mania, but SSRIs (selective serotonin reuptake inhibitors, which help increase levels of mood-boosting serotonin in the brain) like fluoxetine (Prozac or Sarafem) and paroxetine (Seroxat or Paxil) can also cause upward mood swings.

This doesn't mean that antidepressants should be avoided altogether, but they must be taken with extreme care if you have bipolar – usually combined with a mood-stabilising drug like lithium. We'll look in much greater detail at the medications used to treat bipolar disorder in chapter six.

Can anything else cause bipolar disorder?

We've already been through the main things that cause bipolar illness, both genetic and triggers such as the environment we grew up in and lifestyle factors such as sleep-deprivation or drug-taking. But there are some less common factors that we still need to be aware of.

Positive stress

It's clear that negative stressors like bereavement, relationship breakdown or chronic stress at work can act as triggers, both for the onset of illness and mood swings. But some people find that positive life events, such as getting married, having a baby or a major wedding anniversary can also be triggers.

Of course, these events are part and parcel of a happy, well-rounded life, so they should be enjoyed to the full. But it's worth bearing in mind that they can act as triggers, so both the build-up and event itself need to be managed carefully.

Pregnancy

For women with bipolar, there is a very strong correlation between childbirth and having a manic episode. There is particular risk of a condition called 'puerperal psychosis' (or 'postnatal psychosis'), where symptoms of confusion, hallucinations and a disconnection from reality can come on suddenly.

This doesn't mean that women with bipolar should not have children – far from it. But it does mean that this period needs to be managed carefully. Professor Craddock explains: 'Childbirth is one of the biggest triggers for manic episodes. A woman who has had bipolar episodes in the past has a very high risk of mania after childbirth – as much as a one in two risk. So it's important to discuss the possible risk with your family, GP and psychiatrist.'

Puerperal psychosis can be treated with antipsychotic medication, which will nip the symptoms in the bud. That's why it's so important to keep a close eye on your behaviour if you are pregnant and have a history of bipolar disorder.

Seasonal affective disorder (SAD)

If you live in a Northern European country like the UK, you may well suffer from seasonal affective disorder (SAD). It affects around a million people in the UK between September and April, and is thought to result from the lack of bright light during the winter months. December, January and February are especially difficult for SAD sufferers.

Unsurprisingly, if you suffer from depression or bipolar disorder, these months may well be especially difficult for you. The lack of light is thought to cause a biochemical imbalance in a part of the brain called the hypothalamus, which regulates mood, appetite, sleep, temperature and sex drive. That's thought to be a reason why people with SAD sleep more and crave carbohydrate-rich 'comfort foods' like pizza, crisps or cake during these dark months.

It's also thought that, rather than being a separate condition, SAD is a seasonal pattern for people with depression or bipolar disorder – as many as 38% of people with mood disorders are believed to have seasonal variation in symptoms. If this includes you, there are a number of things you can do to cheer yourself up when the days are short and gloomy. We'll look in detail at those in chapter 8.

Summing Up

It's still not clear exactly what causes bipolar disorder, but it seems to be related to an imbalance in our brain chemistry. Research is currently focusing on the role of hormones and neurotransmitters such as serotonin, variants in key genes, the structure of our brain cells and problems with our body clock. What is clear is that bipolar disorder is influenced by a genetic predisposition, because the illness runs in families. You are more likely to become bipolar if one of your parents has the illness, and even more likely if both do.

Even if you do inherit genes that make you vulnerable to developing bipolar illness, it takes a combination of your environment – especially in your early childhood – and a stressful life event, such as a relationship breakdown or bereavement, to trigger the illness. Other triggers include your lifestyle, drugs – both recreational drugs like cocaine or alcohol and prescription drugs such as antidepressants – positive stressors like marriage or a major birthday, pregnancy and childbirth. There is also a close link between the seasons and bipolar disorder, especially the lack of bright light during the winter months.

Chapter Three

Getting a Diagnosis

If you have bipolar disorder, it's extremely important to get a diagnosis as early as possible. This is because the earlier you are diagnosed, the earlier doctors can start treating your illness and the better the long-term outcome will be. Experts believe it's much easier to treat someone who has had fewer than three episodes, because after that bipolar disorder gets incrementally more difficult to treat after each episode.

Unfortunately, this is not the case for most people with bipolar disorder, for reasons we explain later in this chapter. It can take years to get diagnosed and usually requires a severe manic episode before mental health professionals recognise your bipolar illness. The most important thing is to get that diagnosis and then to learn as much as you can about the illness and your treatment – both from mental health professionals and the many things you can do for yourself.

How does someone usually get diagnosed?

Most people with bipolar disorder experience one or more depressive episodes before they ever experience a manic one. This makes it extremely difficult for a correct diagnosis to be made, and is one of the main reasons bipolar is often diagnosed as unipolar depression. Professor Nick Craddock, head of the Cardiff University Psychiatry Service, explains: 'Very often, a person's first episode or episodes will be depression rather than mania. Typically, they will first have been told they have depression and it will only be recognised as bipolar disorder when they have a severe high, which often requires hospitalisation or gets them in trouble with the police. It will then be obvious they are bipolar, so a correct diagnosis can be made.'

'I'd never heard the word before, but for the first time, at the age of 37, I had a diagnosis that explains the massive highs and miserable lows I've lived with all my life.'

Stephen Fry.

This also means it's very rare for your GP to diagnose you with bipolar – he or she will either misdiagnose the illness as depression, or refer you on to a psychiatrist. They will ask you a number of questions that will help them decide if you have bipolar disorder and work out what treatments will help you best – this is called an assessment.

The questions will cover events or feelings leading up to your illness, whether other members of your family have bipolar disorder and whether you have thought about harming yourself or others. The psychiatrist may also talk to a member of your family, but should ask for your agreement first.

Will you have to stay in hospital?

You should receive most of your treatment without having to stay in hospital. But if your symptoms are very severe, or you are being treated under the Mental Health Act, you might be admitted to hospital. If you are experiencing severe mental distress and refusing treatment, or doctors think you might pose a danger to yourself or someone else, you may be 'sectioned'. This means you are compulsorily admitted to hospital for treatment.

But doctors would only section you when it is absolutely necessary to do so – the vast majority of patients are treated with their consent. And you may be offered treatment in a day hospital, where you will spend most of the day but return home at night.

How does the psychiatrist know if it's mania?

The psychiatrist will compare your symptoms with the list in the *Diagnostic and Statistical Manual of Mental Disorders*, or DSM IV (or a similar list in the International Classification of Diseases, version 10, or ICD10). This gives a number of criteria that must be met before a disorder is classified as mania. The first one is that your mood must be elevated, expansive or irritable and the mood must be different to your usual 'affective' (emotional) state when you are stable. There must be a marked change over a period of time, you must become very elevated and have grandiose ideas, and you may also become irritated and appear 'arrogant' in manner.

The second main criteria emphasises that at least three of the following symptoms must be present to a significant degree:

- Inflated sense of self-importance.

- Decreased need for sleep.

- Increased talkativeness.

- Flights of ideas or racing thoughts.

- Easily distracted.

- Increased goal-directed activity.

- Excessive involvement in activities that can bring pleasure but may have disastrous consequences (e.g. sexual affairs or spending excessively).

The third criterion for mania in the DSM-IV states that the change in mood must affect your job performance or relationships with other people. This is used to emphasise the difference between mania (more severe symptoms) and hypomania (milder ones).

Some of the questions a psychiatrist might ask you to see if you have mania are:

- Do you have periods of high energy and productivity?

- How happy or angry do you get and for how long?

- Do you ever have times when you feel you're the best at everything?

- Have you ever got into trouble during these times by spending or borrowing too much money?

- Do your thoughts feel hyperactive?

- Do you sleep too little?

- Do you ever hear voices or believe you have magical powers?

What about depression?

The DSM-IV states that there are a number of criteria by which major depression (as opposed to mild or moderate depression) is clinically defined. You must have experienced the depression for at least two weeks and must have five of the following symptoms:

- A depressed mood for most of the day, almost every day.
- A loss of interest or pleasure in almost all activities, almost every day.
- Changes in weight and appetite.
- Sleep disturbance.
- A decrease in physical activity.
- Fatigue and loss of energy.
- Feelings of worthlessness or excessive feelings of guilt.
- Poor concentration levels.
- Suicidal thoughts.

Both the depressed mood and a loss of interest in everyday activities must form two of the five symptoms for it to be diagnosed as major depression. The psychiatrist may also ask a number of other questions to determine your anxiety level, your mental health history and your lifestyle.

And psychosis?

Not everyone with bipolar disorder will experience psychosis, but it can occur during a severe manic episode. It's characterised by disorders in basic perceptual, cognitive, affective and judgemental processes (in other words, the way you perceive, think about, feel and judge things). If you experience psychosis this may include delusions, hallucinations, or disorganised speech and behaviour. The psychiatrist will ask you questions during the assessment to check whether you have experienced any of these things – if so, he or she will prescribe an anti-psychotic medication which will help reduce or completely eliminate your symptoms (see chapter 6).

What is schizoaffective disorder?

This is defined by the DSM-IV as 'the presence of psychotic symptoms in the absence of mood changes for at least two weeks in a person who has a mood disorder'. It's a diagnosis that is used when someone does not have either typical schizophrenia or a typical mood disorder (illnesses in which someone's mood is the main underlying feature, like major depression or bipolar disorder), but rather has features of both schizophrenia and mood disorder.

Because schizoaffective disorder is such a complex illness, it can be very hard to diagnose – and is often misdiagnosed as bipolar disorder. Ask your psychiatrist or another member of your mental health team if you feel these symptoms are similar to your own.

Case study

Chris, a former teacher and now writer and broadcaster, was originally diagnosed with unipolar depression – a very common misdiagnosis, because most people with bipolar disorder experience several depressive episodes before one of mania. He also explains how finally getting a correct diagnosis was a massive relief, because it helped him to understand the swings between huge success and subsequent failure which had dominated his life.

'I was originally diagnosed with unipolar depression in 1998. After a year off work, I was pensioned off from my job as deputy head of a catholic school in Southend. I was prescribed Prozac, but I suffered badly on it and became very ill. That ended up destroying my first marriage.

'About five years after the misdiagnosis, which was from a private hospital, I went to see an NHS consultant. He took my history and said he didn't think I had unipolar depression at all, and that I had been a manic depressive my whole life.

'That was a great relief to me, because it explained the pattern of my life, which had been enormous successes followed by enormous failures. It was as if I had an unerring capacity both to achieve and to press the self-destruct button, which I think is fairly typical of manic depressives.

'Once I got the new diagnosis, through a combination of new medication and psychotherapy, I became very much better. So the last five years have been an increasingly improving picture. We've now hit on a drugs regime – sodium valproate and Lamotrigine, both mood stabilisers, plus Duloxetine, an antidepressant – that keeps me stable, stops me being suicidal or dangerously manic.'

What questions should I ask?

According to the NICE (National Institute for Health and Clinical Excellence) clinical guidelines on bipolar disorder (see book list), these are some useful questions for you or your family to ask healthcare professionals. If you have already been diagnosed, don't worry – these questions will be useful for you to ask at any time:

- What makes you think I have bipolar disorder?
- What do you think causes my bipolar disorder?
- Are all of my symptoms caused by bipolar disorder?
- How might bipolar disorder affect my everyday life and what might it mean for my physical health?
- How can I recognise the early warning signs of an episode of mania or depression?

Your rights as a patient

It's very important that you and your family are clear about the kind of treatment you are entitled to once you have received a diagnosis. This is especially true as, like any other illness, whether physical or mental, NHS provision for bipolar disorder does vary depending on where you live in the UK. According to the NICE guidelines, here's what you should expect:

'Your treatment and care should take into account your personal needs and preferences, and you have the right to be fully informed and to make decisions in partnership with your healthcare team. To help with this, your healthcare team should give you information you can understand and that is relevant to your circumstances. All healthcare professionals should treat you with respect, sensitivity and understanding and explain bipolar disorder and the treatments for it simply and clearly.'

What support can you expect from healthcare professionals?

As we have seen, it's really important that you and your family know as much as possible about what you can expect once a diagnosis has been made. This is partly because, as with all illnesses, knowledge is power when it comes to managing bipolar symptoms. But getting a diagnosis can be a very worrying experience. Although it helps explain some of the things you will have been thinking and feeling, the fact that bipolar disorder is a lifelong condition which can never actually be cured, only managed, is frightening for some people.

Others are angry or upset about having being labelled as mentally ill, and worry about the effect this will have on the way people will think about and treat them. That's why you have a right to as much information and support as possible from the healthcare professionals who will be looking after you.

The NICE guidelines (which serve as a guide for everyone working for the NHS) state that: 'Your healthcare professional should give you general advice about coping with your symptoms, such as how to spot the early warning signs of an episode and how to sleep well and have a regular lifestyle. They should also tell you about self-help groups and support groups.'

Providing this kind of information will help you make informed decisions about your care. But if you experience very severe symptoms you might not be able to make those decisions or communicate your needs. Just in case you are ever in this position, you can draw up a set of written instructions, called 'advanced directives', explaining exactly which treatments and other help you do or do not want. Your mental health team can help you write these instructions.

NICE adds that if you have had a manic episode or severe depression, your healthcare professional should meet with you again within one week of your first assessment. After that they should see you regularly: every 2-4 weeks in the first three months and then at longer intervals if the treatment is helping.

Who will treat you?

Most people with bipolar disorder receive most of their treatment from a community mental health team (CMHT) which commonly includes a psychiatrist, community psychiatric nurse (CPN), social worker, occupational therapist (OT), clinical psychologist and pharmacist. But your GP will still play a key role in your treatment, so you should ask for an appointment with a psychiatrist if you move to a new GP practice. You should also be offered an appointment if your symptoms become a lot worse, if you are thought to be a risk to yourself or others, if your treatment is not working or if you have drug or alcohol problems.

Ideally, you should be treated by the same healthcare professionals and you should have regular appointments. If you are treated by a number of different healthcare professionals, there should be a clear plan about what each of them does for you.

Why is bipolar misdiagnosed?

It's thought that up to 70% of people with bipolar are initially misdiagnosed and there is, on average, an eight-year delay before a correct diagnosis is made. This is clearly far from ideal. As we have seen, bipolar disorder is often misdiagnosed as major depression, but psychiatrists may also think you have schizophrenia if you are experiencing psychotic symptoms. New research from the University of Texas Health Science Center claims that about one in three people diagnosed with major depression may actually have bipolar disorder. The researchers suggested that five characteristics would help determine whether the depression was in fact bipolar. These were:

* A family history of mania.

* Having at least two mood episodes in the past.

* Occurrence of first psychiatric symptoms before the age of 30.

* A switch to extreme mood swings.

* Mixed states in which symptoms of mania and depression occur together.

Other studies suggest that up to 40% of patients receive another diagnosis first, and that it can take years before they are correctly diagnosed.

The danger here is that if you are misdiagnosed with major depression, you may well be prescribed antidepressants. If you have bipolar, taking antidepressants on their own may not help and can cause you to become manic.

A spectrum disorder

To understand why misdiagnosis is so common, it's useful to remember that bipolar is a 'spectrum disorder', with symptoms ranging from one percent (very mild) to 100 (very severe). At the lower end of this spectrum, you might swing between very mild depression and hypomania. If this doesn't cause any problems in your work or personal life, there's no need to seek treatment – in fact, hypomania can be a real asset, especially for those in the creative industries who thrive on bursts of energy and creativity.

On this spectrum, you can also see bipolar merging with 'normality', with depression and with schizophrenia, as Professor Craddock explains: 'We all have experience of mood varying and sometimes we're much more down than at others. And there are lots of people in the general population who might have severe ups and downs that don't cause a problem, so it would be silly to see that as an illness. It's only when it becomes very severe and disabling that we would talk about it being an illness.'

This all makes it clear just why bipolar is so hard to diagnose, even for the most experienced psychiatrist. Unfortunately, there isn't much they can do if you have only ever experienced depression – or, which is very common, you have experienced mild highs but enjoyed the energy and self-confidence, so wouldn't have thought of telling your GP.

Researchers are working hard to improve the methods available for diagnosis and treatment. In the meantime, if you suspect you might have been misdiagnosed, talk to your GP or psychiatrist.

Summing Up

It's very important to diagnose bipolar disorder as early as possible. The earlier the diagnosis is made, the sooner treatment can begin, and the more effective that treatment will be. Because most people experience one or more episodes of depression before mania, bipolar disorder is commonly misdiagnosed as major depression.

It's often only when someone has a severe manic episode – which may require hospitalisation or involve the police – that a correct diagnosis can be made. This will involve a psychiatrist, who will carry out an assessment, asking questions about your family history of mental illness and lifestyle, as well as questions to determine whether you have experienced depression, mania, anxiety or psychosis.

Once a diagnosis has been made you will be treated by a team of mental health professionals and you have a right to expect that this treatment will be of a high standard. Having as much information as possible about bipolar disorder and its treatment will help you and your family make sure that you get the best possible help and support.

Chapter Four

Depression: the Lows

Many people with bipolar disorder say they enjoy the early stages of a manic episode. They feel confident, energetic and brimming with self-belief. The world looks sparkly and full of exciting possibilities. None would say the same about depression. The low end of the bipolar cycle can be a dark, lonely and deeply unhappy place. It's like the mirror image of mania, with all confidence stripped away and the world drained of all colour.

Although bipolar depression is not exactly the same as unipolar depression (people with bipolar are likely to sleep more, rather than less, for example), the basic thoughts, feelings and overall experience are very similar. And that low mood is all too common, in the UK and across the globe. Mental health charity MIND estimates that one in four of us will suffer some form of mental distress at some point in our lives, most commonly anxiety or depression.

Being depressed is increasingly recognised as a part of the human condition: a darkness that engulfs us, often in response to a life crisis such as bereavement, divorce or unemployment. Some experts argue that depression is now such a fundamental part of our vocabulary, we actually overuse it, 'pathologising' (defining as illness) perfectly natural responses like sadness or grief, which will ease with time.

But in major or bipolar depression, the experience is much worse than mild sadness or feeling a bit down in the dumps. It goes on for longer and makes it extremely difficult to carry on with everyday activities like working, relating to other people or looking after children. At its most severe, depression can be completely disabling, making us feel isolated and deeply unhappy. The good news is that doctors have never understood depression so well, nor have we had such an array of powerful tools to help us feel better.

'I just couldn't get out of bed. I had zero energy. Everything went dark. I was thinking to myself, "Why should I bother getting up? I can't solve any problems anyway, I'm incapable of doing anything."'

Former Norwegian Prime Minister, Kjell Magne Bondevik.

Why do we get depressed?

There are many different theories about why we become depressed and how best to treat it. Some experts see depression – particularly as part of bipolar – as a biological condition, involving chemical imbalances in the brain which profoundly affect the way we think, feel and act. Others argue that it's solely down to our upbringing. They claim that wounds inflicted in infancy and early childhood are to blame, and are less interested in the brain's physical make-up than the relationship we had with our parents.

But most experts on depression, whatever their theoretical approach, now agree that a subtle combination of brain chemistry, our upbringing and childhood environment, stressful or difficult events in later life and, crucially, the way we think about those events, combine to make us depressed.

They therefore call it a 'biopsychosocial' disease – a slightly scary-sounding word that basically means we need to understand not just the bodily and mental aspects of depression but also the interaction between our biology and bodily processes, our psychology and the circumstances in which we live.

Clinical psychologist Dorothy Rowe, one of the world's leading experts on depression, argues that we become depressed because of the way we view the world and, especially, the harsh and critical way we view ourselves. Her book, *Depression: The Way Out of Your Prison* (see book list), has brought comfort to thousands of readers since it was first published in 1983. In it, Rowe describes depression as 'a prison where you are both the suffering prisoner and the cruel jailer'.

There is no doubt that the way we think about ourselves, and the way we perceive the things that happen to us as we move through life, are key aspects of why we get depressed. If you have bipolar disorder, learning more about 'depressive thinking' will help you avoid getting down in the first place and will help lift you out of those dark places when you do get down. We'll look at ways of challenging negative, self-critical thinking in chapter 7.

What is depression?

Perhaps the first thing to say is that, although we have just started talking about it openly in the past few decades, depression is certainly not new. In fact, it has affected humans for as long as records have been kept. It was first named as a condition by ancient Greek doctor Hippocrates, who called it 'melancholia' (the same term later used by Freud).

Experts distinguish between mild-to-moderate and major depression, which used to be called 'endogenous' depression (meaning from within, rather than reacting to a distressing life event). The difference between milder and more severe forms of depression depends on how deeply you experience a common range of symptoms. We referred to these in chapter 1, but as a reminder, they are:

- Feelings of unhappiness that won't go away.

- Feeling that you want to burst into tears for no apparent reason.

- Losing interest in things and being unable to enjoy them.

- Feeling restless, agitated and irritable.

- Losing self-confidence.

- Feeling useless, inadequate and hopeless.

- Negative thinking and thoughts of suicide.

- Finding it hard to concentrate or make decisions.

- Losing appetite and weight.

- Difficulty getting to sleep and waking earlier than usual.

- Feeling exhausted.

- Loss of libido.

- Feeling isolated and avoiding contact with others.

As a rule, the more of these symptoms you have, the more severe your depression is likely to be.

Why depression is about much more than mood

Paul Gilbert is professor of clinical psychology at the University of Derby and another leading expert on depression. In his book *Overcoming Depression: A Self-Help Guide Using Cognitive Behavioral Techniques* (see book list), Professor Gilbert makes the point that depression is much more than just a low mood. He notes that depression affects not only the way we feel, but how we think about things, our energy levels, concentration, sleep, even our libido. Professor Gilbert says depression affects us in a host of different ways.

First, it drains our motivation to do things. We often feel exhausted and apathetic – nothing seems worth the effort. Every day turns into a struggle of forcing ourselves to do the simplest things – with severe depression, even washing or getting out of bed becomes impossible.

Second, we lose the ability to experience pleasure. Life seems empty and joyless. But although we struggle to experience positive feelings and emotions, we can feel more negative emotions, such as anger. Especially for men, depression seems to manifest itself as anger, irritability and frustration. We often lash out at those we love, like our partner or children – we then feel guilty about that, which can make us more depressed, so it's a vicious cycle.

Professor Gilbert also says depression affects our behaviour, relationships, our bodies and, crucially, our thinking. As well as affecting our ability to concentrate and remember things, depression makes us focus on the negatives in life. We may become highly self-critical of ourselves and others, and feel we are 'inferior, flawed, bad or worthless'.

It's absolutely crucial that you remember you are not bad or a failure just because you have depression. It affects millions of people around the world and is not your fault – no more than having asthma or eczema is your fault. You have probably experienced some very difficult things in your life, and depression is a reaction to those difficulties. Don't beat yourself up!

Feeling isolated and alone

One of the hardest things about being depressed is that we can feel cut off from the outside world, unable to reach out and tell people that we need help. In severe depression, we may find it impossible to communicate even with our closest friends and family members. Sufferers often describe depression as being behind a thick Perspex wall: we can see the world around us but feel completely separate, unable to break through and be with everyone else.

One of the great ironies about being depressed is that, not only do we find it hard to ask for help, we may even drive people away when we need them most. Like other aspects of bipolar, depression is tough on everyone involved. You may find that people are unsympathetic, telling you to 'pull your socks up' or 'just cheer up a bit'. As if it were that easy!

Often, people may act this way because they don't understand and feel frustrated because they can't fix it for you or provide simple solutions. If that happens, perhaps you could ask them to read a book like this one, or talk to your family doctor to find out more about depression and bipolar.

And try to resist the urge to pull the duvet over your head and hide away. Along with medication and talking therapies, one of the best ways to combat depression is to be around other people, to get help and support. Many people with bipolar find online forums like Bipolar4all (www.bipolar4all.co.uk) a great way to connect with others who understand what you're going through. See the help list for more details.

Depression and suicide

Sadly, suicide is a very real threat for people with all types of psychiatric illness, and bipolar in particular. According to the NHS Choices website (www.nhs.uk), research has shown that the risk for people with bipolar disorder is 15-20 times more than the general population. And studies have shown that as many as 25-50% of people with bipolar disorder attempt suicide at least once during their lifetime. That's why it's vital that you and those who care about you take this risk seriously. One of the best ways to keep yourself safe is to learn all about the triggers and warning signs for suicide.

If you are bipolar, the risk of suicide is greatest during a depressed or mixed episode. Mental health charity MIND (www.mind.org.uk) warns that this risk is especially high when someone who has been suffering from depression is just beginning to recover. They may have the energy to kill themselves that they lacked when deep in depression. And someone who has thought about suicide in the past, however vaguely, is more likely to resort to it when life becomes stressful.

MIND also gives this list of warning signs:

- Feelings of failure, loss of self-esteem, isolation and hopelessness.

- Sleep problems, particularly waking up early.

- A sense of uselessness and futility. Feeling 'what's the point?'.

- Taking less care of themselves; for example, eating badly or not caring what they look like.

- Suddenly making out a will or taking out life insurance.

- Talking about suicide. It's a myth that people who talk about suicide don't go through with it. In fact, most people who have taken their own lives have spoken about it to someone.

- A marked change of behaviour. Someone may appear to be calm and at peace for the first time or, more usually, may be withdrawn and have difficulty communicating.

Why do people become suicidal?

The reasons that people with bipolar disorder might consider suicide are similar to the reasons anyone might think about ending their life. You may have had a run of problems or bad luck; you might have had a sudden personal crisis, like the end of a relationship that meant a great deal to you; or you may just have been worn down by years of pressures and hurts. Some experts also believe suicide is closely linked to anger, especially unexpressed anger you turn against yourself.

If you are bipolar, delusional ideas may also contribute to suicidal thoughts. For example, you may hear voices telling you to kill yourself. You may have been upset by your diagnosis of bipolar disorder, and feel overwhelmed by the idea that the illness is a lifelong condition.

Alcohol and drug abuse also increase the risk of suicide, especially in young men. And men are much more likely to take their own lives than women – the highest rate of suicide is in men aged 15-44 with men are four times more likely to kill themselves than women. Unemployment is another big factor – attempted suicide is much higher among the unemployed than those who are working.

According to MIND, some people just have a strong desire to die, especially when they feel hopeless about the future and that things will never get better. When the world looks so bleak, suicide can feel like the only way out, especially if life just seems too painful.

But often, even if people have attempted suicide, MIND says: 'They may less want to die than to escape an impossible situation, to relieve an unbearable state of mind, or to convey desperate feelings to others.'

The key point, though, is that, even if people are confused about what they want or which action to take, their life is still at risk. If you are contemplating suicide, please speak to your GP or mental health professional, call Samaritans on 08457 90 90 90 (someone will listen to you and help you work through your difficulties, and the line is open 24 hours a day) or email jo@ samaritans.org

Case study

Martin, 40, explains how painful bipolar depression can be and how severely it affects his relationships, even with the people closest to him. He also makes it clear how easily depressive thoughts can turn to suicide.

'For me it's not as you would imagine. Life can be great and everything is well – relationships, friends, everything, then somewhere deep inside is this blackness that takes over. You just don't want to be around those who love you and you end up hurting them. I found myself telling those close to me that all I wanted was to be under the ground.

'I would spend days in bed, not wash or eat, then I would get paranoid that everyone I knew hated me – and why wouldn't they? I hated me. The depression in my case could last for weeks, sometimes months, causing total destruction to relationships. We often think of depression as a feeling of sadness but with bipolar and my depression that sadness becomes more – it eats away at your very core and you have no control.

'It's like someone has taken away my ability to show emotion – you see things you love, like family, partner, friends, and you just don't want them there. I even asked my partner at the time to kill me and I've asked doctors to help me die.

That was my way of asking for help and it must be very hard for other people to understand, but to me it seemed like the best way.'

In an emergency

If you are trying to help someone who is feeling suicidal, your main concern will be their immediate safety and what's causing them to feel so desperate. So it's important to encourage them to talk about their despairing feelings. Don't dismiss it as a 'cry for help' or try to gee them up. Talking openly about suicide will not make it more likely to happen. Just being there for them and listening in an accepting way, giving them a hug and showing them they are not alone, can make a huge difference.

Persuade them to get some help and outside support, starting with their GP. Discuss strategies for seeking help if they feel suicidal in the future and create a personal support list with the names, phone numbers, websites and addresses of individuals, helplines, organisations and professionals who can help. Persuade the person you are concerned about to keep this list by the phone and get them to agree to call someone if they are feeling suicidal.

As a last resort, if you feel someone is in real danger of killing themselves, has a mental health problem and won't approach anyone for help, you can contact social services. Under the Mental Health Act 1983, someone can be treated without their consent.

If you are in a close relationship with someone who is suicidal, you are likely to feel powerful emotions like fear, anger and guilt. You are likely to need support of your own from a friend, family member, professional or carers' support group – see the help list for details.

Summing Up

Depression, the low end of the bipolar cycle, can be extremely difficult. If you have depression you are likely to have a very low mood, lasting anything from a few days to months on end. You may feel drained and hopeless, as if even the smallest daily tasks get on top of you, and work, socialising with friends or looking after children may prove extremely challenging.

There are many theories about why we get depressed, but, as with bipolar, generally it's likely to be a combination of the genes we inherit, our childhood experiences and stressful events in later life. Experts agree that your thinking – both the way you think about yourself and the way you perceive the world – is a key factor in whether you get depressed or not.

When you are down your thinking is also likely to be affected. You may find it hard to concentrate or remember things, and have unusually negative or self-critical thoughts. Depression also affects your ability to enjoy life and your emotions, draining away the positive ones and making you feel angry and irritable. It can also leave you feeling isolated and alone, cut off from those you care about.

Finally, there is a strong risk of suicide when you are depressed, in a 'mixed' state or just emerging from depression. This is something you and those who care about you must take seriously. As well as learning about the warning signs of suicide, if you feel there is an imminent risk it's vital that you tell someone close to you and contact your GP.

The key message is that the best way to look after yourself, whether you are just down or are worried for your own safety, is by seeking help and support. When you are depressed, it can be tempting to withdraw from the world – but that's never a good idea. Remember that people love and care about you and that, with help and support, you will emerge from your low place and feel much better.

Chapter Five

Mania ≠ hypomania (not a manic) + hypomania and then slowly into psychosis / according to

Mania: the Highs

We all have times where we feel more happy, upbeat, excitable and energetic than others. But if you have bipolar disorder, those feelings can escalate until you barely need to sleep, are talking so fast people find it hard to understand you, are bursting with energy and believe you can do anything, from learning Ancient Greek in a weekend to writing a bestseller or launching a website that will outsell Amazon. Some people have described this escalation, from happy and upbeat to delirious and super-energetic, as being like a runaway train: it starts rolling slowly along the tracks, but because it has no brakes it goes faster and faster until it's speeding out of control.

Milder bouts of heightened energy and mood are called 'hypomania'. This is extremely common – in fact, experts believe that a significant proportion of the population experience hypomania, especially in creative industries like advertising, the media and the performing arts. But in bipolar, if left unchecked these 'hypomanic' symptoms can quickly escalate into mania, which is far more troublesome and extreme.

Some – although not all – people with bipolar will also experience psychosis, when the mania becomes so extreme that they lose touch with reality, have delusional thinking or even hallucinate, hearing voices and seeing things that aren't really there.

> 'Seven years ago I had an attack of pathological enthusiasm. I believed I could stop cars and paralyse their forces by merely standing in the middle of the highway with my arms outspread.'
>
> Robert Lowell, Pulitzer Prize-winning poet.

What happens during a manic episode?

Like every aspect of bipolar disorder, the exact symptoms you experience during a manic episode, how severe they are and how long they last will be unique to you. But there are some common experiences that people with bipolar describe. The Royal College of Psychiatrists' website (www.rcpsych. ac.uk) describes mania as 'an extreme sense of wellbeing, energy and optimism. It can be so intense that it affects your thinking and judgement. You may believe strange things about yourself, make bad decisions, and behave in embarrassing, harmful and – occasionally – dangerous ways.'

We ran through the most common symptoms of mania – as listed in the DSM-IV, in chapter 1. As a reminder, they are:

- Feeling very happy and excited.
- Getting irritated with others who don't share your optimistic outlook.
- Feeling more important than usual.
- Bursting with new and exciting ideas.
- Moving quickly from one idea to another.
- Being full of energy.
- Being unable or unwilling to sleep.
- Having an increased interest in sex.
- Making grandiose and unrealistic plans.
- Being very active and moving around quickly.
- Behaving strangely.
- Talking very quickly – so that others find it hard to understand you.
- Making odd, impulsive decisions, sometimes with disastrous consequences.
- Spending recklessly.
- Being over-familiar with or hyper-critical of others.
- Being generally less inhibited.

Like depression, mania is not just about a changed mood. These symptoms describe changes in your emotions, thinking, bodily sensations and behaviour. According to the World Health Organisation (WHO), a manic episode can last between two weeks and five months if left untreated.

A key point to make here is that, if you are in the middle of your first manic episode, you may not realise that anything's wrong. Especially at the beginning of the episode, before the train starts speeding out of control; you are likely to feel happy, confident and energetic, with a head full of excited plans. Not exactly a time when you want to visit the GP and tell them you're unwell, is it?

But your family, friends and colleagues almost certainly will realise you are behaving strangely and that something's not quite right. You may well feel offended if they try to point this out, but it's crucial that you listen and heed their advice to get some help, before the episode becomes more severe.

How do manic symptoms develop?

Psychologists believe that mania stems from a vicious cycle of mood, thinking, behaviour and bodily changes, like the one below:

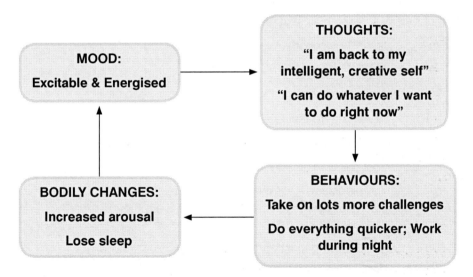

(From clinical psychologist Warren Mansell's factsheet: *What is Bipolar Disorder?*)

These four elements are thought to get more extreme over time, until the person is experiencing mania or hypomania. With cognitive behavioural therapy (CBT), people can learn how to change this cycle by thinking about and responding to their feelings in different ways – for details see chapter 7.

The difference between mania and hypomania

Hypomania is sometimes described as 'mania lite' – many of the symptoms are similar to full-blown mania, but are less extreme. The World Health Organisation describes hypomania as a period when 'the mood is elevated or irritable to a degree that is definitely abnormal for the individual concerned and sustained for at least four consecutive days.'

It is, however, a bit of a grey area and many experts think hypomania is often diagnosed rather than mania, because it sounds more acceptable. Take a look at the DSM-IV's list of symptoms during a hypomanic episode and you will see how closely they resemble its list for mania:

- Feeling exceptionally confident with inflated self-esteem.

- Feeling a need for less sleep, and feeling rested after only a few hours' sleep.

- Being more talkative than usual, or feeling a need to keep talking.

- Feeling full of ideas with racing thoughts.

- Being easily distracted, and darting from one activity to another.

- Increased goal-directed activity.

- Involvement in pleasurable activities that have a high potential for painful consequences (e.g. spending sprees that result in debt, or a sexual encounter that is later regretted).

- Feeling very excited and in a euphoric mood for at least several days on end, which can switch to irritability, intolerance and rage.

- Increased activity and high energy levels.

- Being unusually friendly, seeking out people, including strangers.

- Increased productivity and creativity.

It's also worth noting that hypomania is very common among the general 'healthy' population. Think about everyone you know and a few of them will exhibit at least a few of these symptoms from time to time. As Professor Nick Craddock, head of the Cardiff University Psychiatry Service, says: 'Some people are a bit bubbly and over-exuberant their whole lives, but that's fine. In fact it's good – we need people like that around. The problem comes when it's mixed in with disabling episodes of going over the top or being too low, which clearly isn't good for them or those around them.'

How mania affects behaviour

One of the most difficult aspects of mania is the way it affects your behaviour and decision-making. It can be extremely destructive for relationships, both at work and with friends and loved ones. When someone is manic it can be hard for them to understand the impact their words and actions have on other people – they may feel like the life and soul and be confused that other people don't share their enthusiasm.

During a manic episode you may experience delusions of grandeur and think you know the answers to the world's problems, or can solve the financial and other problems of your friends and family. You may become extremely over-friendly or over-critical, treating complete strangers as if you have known them your whole life. Clearly this can be confusing, at the very least, for the people involved, and can get you into all sorts of trouble.

Risk-taking behaviour of all kinds is associated with manic episodes, as Dr Cosmo Hallstrom, fellow of the Royal College of Psychiatrists, explains: 'I think the ups are most destructive for people with bipolar,' he says. 'People can get into an awful lot of trouble in a very limited period of time. Sexual indiscretions, spending a lot of money, making a fool of themselves in public. It might only last a few days, but living it down can be a long-term process.'

Consequences of mania more destructive according to. [handwritten marginal note]

Mania and sex

As Dr Hallstrom explained, one aspect of manic behaviour that gets people into real trouble is risky sexual behaviour. This can happen because mania increases your energy, confidence and interest in sex (just as depression tends to decrease all of these). This might mean you pursue sexual conquests more aggressively than usual, or misinterpret friendliness as something more.

It may mean you find yourself in dangerous situations – especially if you are a woman – or engage in unprotected sex, so put yourself at risk of contracting an STI (sexually transmitted infection). As we have seen, during a hypomanic or manic phase, you may be unwilling to listen to those concerned about your welfare. But, having read this, remember that those people are only trying to protect you, so try to take their advice on board.

If you have engaged in unprotected sex and are worried you may have an STI, you can get free, confidential advice from your GP or a specialist clinic in your area (even if you're under 16). Most hospitals have special clinics called genito-urinary medicine (GUM) clinics that give tests and treatment for STIs. To find one in your local area visit the NHS Choices website (www.nhs.uk). Or take a look at the Need2Know Book *Sexually Transmitted Infections – The Essential Guide*.

Mania and debt

Over-spending is another major issue for people experiencing a manic episode. A recent MIND report into the link between mental illness and debt, *In the Red: Debt and Mental Health* (see book list) found that people with experience of mental distress were three times more likely to be in debt than the general population – this figure rose to four times for those with bipolar disorder.

A quick glance at the symptoms associated with mania makes it clear why. During a manic episode you might make plans that are grandiose and unrealistic, such as investing in a dubious money-making scheme or starting a business; you might make odd decisions on the spur of the moment, like placing a large bet, buying drinks for a bar full of people or making reckless purchases like a new car, designer clothes or even property.

54

Clearly, having access to large amounts of credit is a bad idea during a manic episode – think about cutting up your cards or asking the credit card company to put a cap on your purchases. Again, try to listen to friendly advice if people express concern about your spending. And if you do find yourself in debt, see the help list for organisations that can help you regain control of your finances.

Case study

Robert Westhead, 36, works for Shift, a campaign against stigmatising mental illness. He describes the extreme episodes of mania he experienced as a teenager, before getting a diagnosis and receiving treatment – and how those episodes spilled over into psychosis

'While travelling abroad during a year off I became seriously ill. I'd been travelling in India and at one point my mood swings started becoming regular and increasingly severe – not ordinary mood swings.

'I would get very down for a week or 10 days, then would suddenly be the life and soul of the party. I remember being in Kashmir and suddenly feeling unaccountably happy, sociable, witty and full of energy.

'When I got home and my parents met me off the plane, I was talking ten to the dozen and telling them I didn't need to sleep – when you're high you become more and more ill and can literally go without sleep. My parents didn't know what to think.

'The illness got more and more extreme. My highs were getting worse and I was losing all sense of reality. I was constantly talking and my speech became so fast I stopped making sense. I was spouting poetry and behaving very oddly, like dashing back to my old school and taking over lessons.

'I also had psychotic delusions, especially religious ones – I thought I was on some kind of mission from God and remember seeing God's face in the smallest things, like a light switch or God staring out at me from cracks in the pavement.'

What is psychosis?

As Robert's story makes clear, sometimes a severe episode of mania can lead to psychosis (meaning a loss of contact with reality). The Royal College of Psychiatrists' website states that, during a manic episode, psychotic symptoms 'tend to be grandiose beliefs about yourself – that you are on an important mission or that you have special powers and abilities'.

You may also experience psychotic symptoms during a depressive episode, such as feeling you are uniquely guilty, worse than everybody else or even that you don't exist. As well as these unusual beliefs, the Royal College's site says: 'You might experience hallucinations – when you hear, smell, feel or see something, but there isn't anything (or anybody) there to account for it'.

It's interesting how often these symptoms involve some kind of religious or spiritual dimension. Like Robert, many people with bipolar think they are on a mission from God to bring about world peace or wipe out poverty. If you have a psychotic episode you may also believe you have superhuman powers, like the ability to read other people's minds. Paranoia is another common problem for people with bipolar, which can make you hyper-sensitive to perceived insults or slights.

Remember that not everyone with bipolar disorder will experience a psychotic episode. But if you do experience any of these symptoms, tell your GP or community mental health team, because they will be able to prescribe medication to relieve your symptoms.

Mixed states

People with bipolar can experience mixed states, in which they experience symptoms of mania and depression at the same time. For example, they might be depressed and agitated at the same time, or have racing thoughts and overactivity (mania), but feel worthless and guilty (depression). Mixed states are extremely common for those with bipolar disorder – it's estimated that around two-thirds of those diagnosed with the illness will suffer at least one mixed episode at some point.

This can be a very dangerous combination of moods, because you may have the suicidal thoughts and feelings associated with depression, but be agitated and energetic enough to put those thoughts into action. Again, if you are in this position please tell your GP or mental health worker.

Is there an upside to mania?

Without in any way downplaying the seriousness of mania, or bipolar disorder in general, it's good to end on a positive – there is an upside. In *You Don't Have to be Famous to Have Manic Depression* (see book list), one of the authors, Jeremy Thomas, says his experiences of bipolar have enriched him: 'The illness provides experiences and a view of the world that those who have not been there can never appreciate.'

He also refers to a survey from the Doctors Support Network (a self-help group for doctors with mental health problems), in which 95% of those questioned found something positive in their experiences. They were more empathic with their patients and had greater self-awareness and maturity.

As we have seen, hypomania is extremely common among creatives like writers, artists and comedians, who may not have created some of the books, plays, works of art and films we all love without periods of heightened creativity and energy.

Summing Up

Everyone has times where they feel happier, more energetic and upbeat than others. But if you have bipolar disorder, these feelings can quickly escalate into hypomania, where you need less sleep, feel exceptionally confident, easily distracted, talkative and euphoric for several days on end. Some people with bipolar disorder (especially Bipolar II), will only ever experience hypomania, periods of stability and depressive episodes.

But for others (especially those with Bipolar I), if untreated, this hypomania can escalate into a full-blown manic episode, where you get irritated with others who don't share your optimism, are bursting with new and exciting ideas, are unwilling to sleep, have an increased interest in sex, behave strangely and make odd, impulsive decisions – often involving risky behaviour to do with sex or spending.

If you are experiencing your first hypomanic or manic episode, you may not realise anything is wrong. After all, who doesn't want to feel more energetic, confident and creative? But your friends, family and colleagues probably will think you're behaving strangely. You may not want to listen to their advice and may become irritable or offended if they suggest you seek help. But they are only looking out for your wellbeing, so it's very important that you listen to their concerns.

Two of the most problematic aspects of mania are risky sexual behaviour and overspending. If you have engaged in unprotected sex, talk to your GP about getting tested for STIs (sexually transmitted infections). And if you are worried about overspending or have got into trouble with money, see the help list for organisations that can help.

Some people with bipolar also experience mixed states, in which they experience symptoms of both mania and depression at the same time. And some also experience psychotic symptoms, when they might see, smell or hear things that aren't there. If either of these happen to you, talk to your GP or mental health worker as soon as possible.

Chapter Six

Which Medications Can Help?

If you have been diagnosed with bipolar disorder, it's very important that you take the medication you are prescribed. This will be invaluable in helping you manage your mood and avoid swinging into severe episodes of depression, mania or psychosis. Unfortunately, as Sarah Nayler's story (overleaf) shows, medication is not a magic bullet – it can take months or even years to get the dosage and combination of different medications exactly right.

It can also be hard to absorb the news that you will have to take medication for the rest of your life. As with diabetes or asthma, doctors cannot cure bipolar disorder, they can only manage its symptoms. But the good news is that their ability to manage those symptoms has come on leaps and bounds in the last few decades. As we have seen, a combination of medication, talking therapies and self-care will help control your symptoms, and minimise both the number and severity of your mood swings.

A key fact to remember here is that, if left untreated or treated ineffectively, bipolar disorder can be damaging to both your mind and body. One reason for this is that people with bipolar disorder (as with other mental illnesses) are more likely to smoke and to abuse alcohol and drugs, or have an eating disorder such as anorexia or bulimia, than the general population. And the rate of coexisting illnesses, such as diabetes and high blood pressure, is also higher among those with bipolar disorder.

'I would go so far as saying that, over the years, medication has saved my life.'
Sarah Nayler.

That's why effective treatment – combining the right medication with things like regular exercise and a healthy diet – will not only improve the quality of your life but could also help you live longer. This is another good reason to seek treatment as early as possible, and then to work closely with your community mental health team to adapt that treatment to your needs.

Also, if you're unhappy with your medication, it's very important that you don't stop taking it suddenly, as this can make you very ill. If you're determined to come off a particular medication that is entirely up to you, but discuss it with your psychiatrist first.

Case study

Sarah Nayler works for a leading mental health charity. Her story is a perfect example of how difficult it can be to get the balance of different medications right – but also how much medication helps when you do find that balance.

'I first had symptoms of mental illness at 15. I changed dramatically from a bubbly, happy-go-lucky teenager to one who was scared of crowded places, panicky, paranoid, depressed and suicidal. I visited my GP on many occasions. He put my experiences down to puberty and teenage problems; however he continued to prescribe medication – antidepressants and mild tranquilisers. But the instability and low mood didn't go away.

'I didn't like taking medication, it made me feel lethargic, shaky and like a zombie – lifeless and numb. Somehow though, I believed that the next pill might help, so I kept trying different tablets.

'One day, things changed dramatically. I was rushing around, talking very quickly, trying to do three things at once and had unstoppable energy, so I was referred to a psychiatrist. He said I had classic signs of manic depression and prescribed me haloperidol, which I had a very bad reaction to. My facial muscles seized up, my jaw locked and I had paralysis down my neck and arm. This was extremely frightening. Luckily, when I was given the antidote in A&E I regained normal movement.

60

'From 16 to 19 my mental health remained unstable and I was given a cocktail of medications and had many hospital admissions. At 20 I reached a place of stability and my life turned around. I remained on an even keel (although fragile) and worked full-time, gained promotions at work and got married.

'Unfortunately, at 28, my mental health took a turn for the worse and I had a severe relapse. I was hospitalised for five months. I hated being on the ward but I knew my medication needed to be assessed.

'I now take several medications including an antidepressant, mood stabiliser, sleeping pill and antipsychotic. I have been on the same drug regime for the past three years and my life is back on track. I would rather be on less medication but at the moment it is helping me enormously. I would go so far as saying that over the years medication has saved my life.

'That said, although bipolar can strike with no rhyme or reason it is greatly affected by life changes and stress – a person's recovery is about so much more than just medication. Although it can play a huge part in someone's life there needs to be a balance of many other factors.'

How medication helps

Depending on your symptoms, you are likely to be prescribed some combination of mood stabilisers, antidepressants, antipsychotics and anti-anxiety drugs. One of these mood stabilisers, lithium, remains the most important drug for treating bipolar disorder, despite being discovered over 60 years ago. Lithium, a naturally occurring salt, works wonders for some people, but can have side effects, especially weight gain.

Unfortunately, as with other medications, there is no way of knowing who will be helped by lithium and who will suffer serious side effects. It seems likely that those most likely to be helped are those with a strong family history of bipolar disorder, and who are fairly stable between episodes.

Again, as with other medications, your psychiatrist will probably start you on a fairly low dose and build this up gradually until he or she has found your optimum level. For detailed information about what lithium and other medications do, when they are prescribed and their possible side effects, see the tables below.

Why is medication so important?

To give you some idea of just how important it is that you keep taking your medication, take a look at table 1. This makes it clear how likely it is that you will have a manic episode without medication – and that the more manic episodes you have had in the past, the greater this risk becomes.

What will happen without medication?

Number of previous manic episodes	Chance of having another episode in the next year	
	Not taking lithium	Taking lithium
1-2	10% (1 in 10)	6-7% (6-7 in 100)
3-4	20% (1 in 5)	12% (12 in 100)
5+	40% (4 in 10)	26% (26 in 100)

Taken from the Royal College of Psychiatrists' leaflet, *Bipolar Disorder (Manic Depression)*.

Why doesn't medication work perfectly every time?

Although doctors have an increasingly sophisticated understanding of how different medications affect our brains, when they first prescribe you a particular medication they can never know exactly how well it will work. This can be extremely frustrating for you – especially if you are still experiencing unpleasant symptoms or side effects – but rest assured that they are doing their absolute best. Try to be patient and give your psychiatrist as much information as possible about your reaction to the medication.

To give you an idea of just how difficult it is to get the dosage right, here's Professor Nick Craddock, head of the Cardiff University Psychiatry Service, again: 'The good news is that we have a number of medications that are proven to be helpful. The bad news is that they're not effective in everybody, and you can't predict who they'll help and who they won't.'

Despite decades of research and thousands of studies, prescribing drugs to treat bipolar disorder is still not an exact science. 'It does boil down to trial and error,' admits Professor Craddock, 'guided by trials and the literature, of course. But if I see someone in clinic, diagnose them with bipolar disorder and say a mood stabiliser will help, even lithium – the most tried and trusted – helps about 70% of people. So I don't know for sure if it will help them or not.'

Again, the good news is that lithium will work for the large majority of people – and even if not, one of the other mood stabilisers should do.

Treatments for episodes of mania or hypomania

The *NICE Guidelines for Carers* explain in detail which medications you will be prescribed to treat mania or hypomania and what you need to know about them. These may include:

- An antipsychotic (such as olanzapine, quetiapine and risperidone). This can be helpful if symptoms are severe or your behaviour is disturbed.

- Lithium. This is normally offered if you have fairly mild symptoms.

- Valproate. This may be offered if it has helped you before – but it's not usually offered to pregnant women because it might harm the baby.

 A benzodiazepine (like Valium or Xanax). This may be offered in addition to an antipsychotic, lithium or valproate, to help you calm down and sleep better.

Medication for depression

If you become depressed while you are already taking medication for mania, your doctor should check that you are taking the right dose and change it if necessary. According to the NICE guidelines, if your symptoms are relatively mild, you will probably not be offered treatment with an antidepressant right away. But your healthcare professional should arrange to see you again, usually within two weeks.

If your symptoms are more severe or have become worse, you may be offered an antidepressant. These work by boosting levels of natural chemicals called neurotransmitters that are found in the brain. Neurotransmitters control or regulate bodily functions and it's thought that depression occurs when nerve cells in the brain don't release enough noradrenalin and serotonin, which regulate mood.

All antidepressants take between two and eight weeks to start having an effect. This means you need to keep taking them, even if they don't seem to make much difference at first. Some people can stop taking the antidepressant as soon as they recover from the depressive episode, but others may have to stay on it for longer, even for months. This will depend on how you have previously responded to antidepressants.

Ideally though, the antidepressant should be stopped as soon as the depressive episode has fully resolved, because there is the risk of triggering a manic or hypomanic episode. And the dose should be tapered off over a period of four weeks.

Here's a list of the most common antidepressants from Netdoctor (www.netdoctor.co.uk):

Selective serotonin reuptake inhibitors (SSRIs)

Cipralex (escitalopram)   Faverin (fluvoxamine)   Prozac (fluoxetine)

Cipramil (citalopram)   Lustral (sertraline)   Seroxat (paroxetine)

- SSRIs have fewer troublesome side effects than the older tricyclics and MAOIs (Monoamine oxidase inhibitors), making them the preferred type of antidepressant for people with bipolar depression.

- SSRIs are less likely than other antidepressants to cause abnormally high mood (mania or hypomania) when used to treat depressive episodes in bipolar disorder.

- SSRIs are less sedating than the older antidepressants and are more suitable for people with heart problems and those who feel slowed up by their depression.

- The most common side effects are gastrointestinal effects, such as nausea, vomiting, diarrhoea and constipation.

- Other side effects include headache, dizziness, agitation and insomnia.

- All antidepressants can be associated with sexual problems such as impotence, but this seems to occur most frequently with the SSRIs.

- Fluoxetine may be used less frequently than other SSRIs because it stays in the body for a long time after treatment is stopped, which could be a problem if treatment needs to be stopped quickly because of a manic episode.

Tricyclic antidepressants (TCAs)

Allegron (nortriptyline)	Anafranil SR (clomipramine)	Prothiaden (dothiepin)
Amitriptyline	Imipramine	Sinepin (doxepin)
Anafranil (clomipramine)	Lomont (lofepramine)	Surmontil (trimipramine)

- Tricyclic antidepressants are only rarely used in bipolar depression because they carry the highest risk of causing sudden switches to mania.

- All TCAs cause drowsiness to varying degrees. Amitriptyline and dothiepin are the most sedating and these may be of benefit to people who are also anxious or agitated. Imipramine and lofepramine are less sedating.

- Other common side effects include constipation, difficulty in urinating, blurred vision, dry mouth and weight gain.

- People with heart disease should not take TCAs.

- Venlafaxine works in a similar way to the TCAs, but does not produce the side effects associated with these antidepressants. However, it also seems to carry a higher risk of causing sudden switches into mania.

Monoamine oxidase inhibitors (MAOIs)

Isocarboxazid	Manerix (moclobemide)
Nardil (phenelzine)	Tranylcypromine

- In general, MAOIs are used far less frequently than the other antidepressants because they interact with certain foods and require strict dietary restrictions.

- MAOIs can also cause severe adverse reactions if taken with many other medicines, including some over-the-counter cough and cold remedies.

- Moclobemide is a newer MAOI and is used more frequently than the older MAOIs. It is believed to cause fewer problems than traditional MAOIs, but caution is still required with certain foods and medicines.

How mood stabilisers and antipsychotics affect you long term

As we have seen, medications affect different people in different ways. The *NICE Guidelines for Carers*, explain in detail what you need to know about the drugs most commonly prescribed for bipolar disorder. Do bear in mind though, that not everyone will have side effects – and even if you do, those effects can range from mild to severe.

With all of these drugs, you should have a number of tests when you start taking the drug and then at regular intervals – ask your doctor for more information. This is a digested version of the common side effects and key points about each type of drug:

- Antipsychotics. You may gain weight and if you are diabetic your condition could get worse. If you are offered quetiapine, start on a low dose and gradually increase it.

- Lithium. Do not miss doses or stop taking the drug suddenly. See a doctor if you have diarrhoea or are vomiting. Drink water regularly, particularly after sweating and if you are over 65, have a chest infection or pneumonia or are immobile for long periods. You should usually avoid taking anti-inflammatory drugs like ibuprofen. Take lithium for at least six months before trying a different drug.

- Valproate. Not normally offered to women if they could get pregnant because there may be risks to an unborn child. Your doctor should tell you how to spot signs of blood or liver problems and what to do if these develop. Your doctor should also be careful if you are also taking a drug for epilepsy, and see you more often if you are over 65.

- Lamotrigine. Your doctor should start you on a low dose and increase it gradually, especially if you are also taking valproate. Seek medical help urgently if you develop a rash. Should not be taken with the contraceptive pill.

- Carbamazepine. Only take carbamazepine after consulting an expert in bipolar disorder. Start on a low dose and increase it gradually. Carbamazepine can cause problems if you are taking other drugs (including the contraceptive pill), so you will need careful checks.

Summing Up

If you have bipolar disorder, it's extremely important that you take medication to manage your mood and help you avoid swings into depression, mania or psychosis. Like asthma or diabetes, bipolar disorder is a lifelong condition, so although it cannot be cured, this medication will help you manage its symptoms. Effective treatment, including medication, could extend your life expectancy.

This medication is likely to be some combination of antidepressants, mood stabilisers, antipsychotics and anti-anxiety drugs. The most commonly prescribed – and still the most effective – drug for bipolar is lithium, a naturally occurring salt that helps stabilise your mood. Lithium is effective for around 70% of people but, like other forms of medication, it may cause side effects ranging from mild to severe.

Despite decades of research, there is still no way of knowing who will find different medications helpful and who will experience side effects. So finding the right dosage and combination of medications for you is a process of trial and error – albeit a highly scientific one. It's vital that you keep taking the medication, as it may take a while to work. And if you are determined to stop taking it at any point, you must do so with your mental health professional's advice and consent, as stopping medication abruptly could cause an episode of depression, mania or hypomania.

Chapter Seven

Talking Therapies

Treating your bipolar disorder involves three main areas. Medication, as we saw in the last chapter, is the first and most important way to tackle your illness. Whatever else you do, remember that taking your medication every day is vital to help keep your symptoms under control. As we will see in the next chapter, learning self-care is also very important – another way in which you can take control of your illness and its impact on your life.

The third approach to treating bipolar is talking therapies, which we will explore here. Talking therapies, as the name suggests, are treatments that involve you talking about your problems to a professional, either one to one or in a group. Extensive research shows that combining medication with talking therapies is much more effective than medication alone, so it's useful for you to understand what the different approaches involve, how effective they are, how long they take and how you can gain access to them, either privately or through the NHS.

'A man is but the product of his thoughts. What he thinks, he becomes.'
Mahatma Gandhi

How do talking therapies help?

On the most basic level, it does us all good to sit down and talk to someone who is kind and compassionate, and listens to us without making judgements or criticising us. All good counsellors and therapists offer this, whatever their background or approach. All the research into what makes therapy work shows that, above all else, the relationship between therapist and client is the most healing part – more than the therapist's skill or experience, and whatever techniques they use.

If you have bipolar disorder, this applies to you as much as everyone else. But you need particular help in managing your mood swings – learning to spot the warning signs as early as possible and then knowing what to do to avoid a full-blown depressive or manic episode. So when you are thinking about which talking therapy might be useful, make sure you choose the one best suited to clients with bipolar disorder.

It's worth noting that psychiatrists used to think bipolar disorder was a purely 'biological' illness, caused solely by imbalances in our brain chemistry and only treatable with medication. But mental health professionals no longer believe this – the evidence proving that talking therapies are effective in managing bipolar disorder is strong and clear.

For example, a long-term study by researchers from the University of Colorado found that adding intensive psychotherapy to a bipolar patient's medication treatment helped the patient recover more rapidly from depression. They were also one-and-a-half times more likely to be 'clinically well' during any month of the study year, compared with those who didn't receive therapy.

Let's now look at the most common talking therapies used to treat bipolar disorder, starting with cognitive behavioural therapy (CBT) – the talking therapy with the strongest evidence base, owing to the large number of well-controlled studies showing it to be effective.

What is CBT?

Cognitive behavioural therapy, or CBT, is receiving a great deal of attention at the moment, because the Department of Health believes it to be the most effective psychological treatment available and is training thousands of CBT therapists under the Improving Access to Therapies (IAPT) programme. Although some psychotherapists feel that other approaches are being neglected in favour of CBT – and that we should be offered a variety of therapies from the NHS to suit our individual needs – a large body of research proves that CBT is effective at treating a number of conditions.

CBT has been shown to help with anxiety, depression, panic, phobias, stress, bulimia, obsessive-compulsive disorder, post-traumatic stress disorder, bipolar disorder and psychosis. It aims to help change how you think ('cognitive') and what you do ('behaviour'), in order to help you feel better. Unlike some other approaches, CBT primarily focuses on your 'here and now' problems and difficulties. Its aim is very much to improve your current state of mind.

Perhaps the key thing to understand about CBT is that it helps change the way you think, especially if the pattern of your thoughts tends to be negative or destructive. Cognitive therapists argue that the way you think impacts on the way you feel, and so affects your mood. This in turn influences the way you act.

CBT breaks overwhelming problems down into smaller parts. This makes it easier to see how they are connected and how they affect you. As you can see from the diagram below, these parts will be: the situation (your boss shouted at you at work); your thoughts ('he hates me and always picks on me'); your feelings (low, sad, angry, frustrated); and action (you felt so bad you took the following day off sick, missing an important presentation).

Clearly, this is an example of unhelpful thoughts, feelings and actions – your therapist will show you how to replace these with more helpful responses – for example, you might think, 'He's clearly having a bad day, but it's not acceptable to shout like that. I'll make that clear to him when he calms down.' This is likely to trigger a whole different set of feelings, such as determination, as you refuse to be bullied and decide to be assertive about it. In turn, if the meeting with your boss goes well, you are unlikely to skip work the next day, and avoid the self-destructive consequences of missing your presentation.

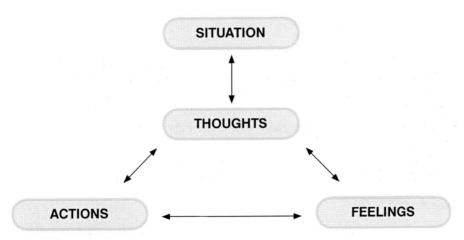

Originally printed in the Royal College of Psychiatrists' leaflet, *Cognitive Behavioural Therapy (CBT)*.

What happens in CBT sessions?

According to the Royal College of Psychiatrists' leaflet on CBT (see book list), you will usually meet with a CBT therapist for between five and 20 weekly or fortnightly sessions, with each session lasting between 30 and 60 minutes. In the first few sessions, the therapist will check that you can use this sort of treatment and that you feel comfortable with it. They will also ask you questions about your life and background – although CBT focuses on the present, you may need to talk about the past to understand how it's affecting you now.

The work itself involves the following:

- You decide what you want to deal with in the short, medium and long term and you and the therapist will usually start each session by agreeing on what to discuss that day.

- With the therapist, you break each problem down into its separate parts. Your therapist may ask you to keep a diary to identify your pattern of thoughts, emotions, bodily feelings and actions.

- Together you will look at those thoughts, feelings and behaviours to work out if they are unrealistic or unhelpful; and how they affect each other and you.

- The therapist will then help you work out how to change unhelpful thoughts and behaviours.

- Your therapist may well give you homework, so you start practising these changes in everyday life.

How CBT can help regulate your moods

One of the reasons CBT is so helpful for people with bipolar disorder is that it's uniquely effective at helping you understand how, when and why you experience mood swings. Warren Mansell, senior lecturer in psychology at the University of Manchester, explains what he focuses on when working with bipolar clients: 'For each individual you work out their cycle of mood escalation and how that impacts on their behaviour and other people. That's not just about identifying individual symptoms, but the whole process of how their mood develops, the relationship between their thoughts, feelings, behaviour and environment that drives their mood into problematic areas.'

Need2Know

This is a key point. People with bipolar tend to explain how they are feeling as being something to do with themselves, rather than their environment. The way that you feel is influenced by a wide range of internal factors, such as negative or self-critical thoughts; and external ones, such as whether your work is stressful and demanding. A good CBT therapist will help you understand how these factors combine to influence your mood.

They will also help you detect early warning signs for your mood swings. For a depressive episode, these might include:

- Negative thoughts.

- Feelings of anxiety.

- A lack of energy.

- Insufficient/interrupted sleep.

- Low motivation and withdrawing from social or enjoyable activities.

- Lack of interest in food or sex.

For a manic episode, early warning signs might include:

- Thoughts starting to race.

- Irritability.

- Heightened sense of self-worth.

- Needing less sleep.

- Feeling overexcited and restless and being more sociable than usual.

- 'Goal-directed' activities like planning a new business or doing a makeover on your house.

- Over-spending.

Once you know your own particular warning signs, it's easier to take action to make sure your mood swings don't escalate into a full-blown manic or depressive episode. But, as Warren Mansell explains, it's also important to learn that some variation in mood is completely normal. 'One of the key aims of CBT therapy with bipolar clients is normalising ups and downs – that means teaching them that the mood itself isn't the problem, it's how they think about the mood. So if you feel a bit hyped and overactive for a few hours after something great has happened, that feeling itself isn't a problem.'

He adds that problems start when these moods escalate, leading to unusual or unhelpful behaviours. 'If you then think, "This means I can achieve everything I ever wanted," and start phoning everyone you know and persuading them to sign up to some grand scheme, then that could be more of a problem. So it is how these feelings and thoughts build up and escalate that drives the problem with moods, and CBT helps people notice this cycle and learn ways to step outside it.'

Remember: everyone has changeable moods. It's only when those moods, or the actions they lead to, become a problem for you or those around you, that you need to get help with them.

Case study

Jonathan Naess worked as a lawyer in the City before leaving to set up Stand to Reason, a charity that tackles the stigma associated with mental illness. He describes how CBT has helped him manage his bipolar disorder.

'When I'm depressed, I find it really hard to get out of bed and find it difficult to do anything constructive. So a lot of my initial work with a CBT therapist was on simple, practical stuff, just to get me moving again and slowly build up some momentum. I'm a real perfectionist and give myself a very hard time if I'm not doing a million things every day, so the therapist taught me to lower my expectations and allow myself to do just two or three things in a day.

'I can also get very isolated when I'm depressed – I could easily not leave the house for a week. So another key thing we worked on was making sure I saw people, actually putting that in my diary so I saw at least one person a day. I was really struggling at the time, so breaking it down into simple steps, doing small constructive things, did help lift me out of my depression.

'Another thing we worked on was having at least one thing every week to look forward to. I couldn't even think about doing vigorous exercise, but I was just about up to a round of golf. That gave me something enjoyable to focus on too.

'Once we had worked on that behavioural stuff, we worked on my thinking patterns. I began to see that the language I used about myself was very negative. So I learned that being kind to myself was very important, instead of judging myself so harshly, because, of course, that brings you down. It's a vicious circle you need to interrupt.

'As well as the CBT work, I also found the self-help groups run by MDF – the BiPolar Organisation really useful. Talking to people who have the empathy for you that you don't have for yourself helps to interrupt the dreadful rumination – I get so exhausted of the same thoughts going round and round my head. So a combination of the therapy with the self-group helped cut through that, which lifted me out of my depression.'

Family-focused therapy

Family-focused therapy (FFT) is another talking treatment commonly used to treat bipolar disorder. It's a hybrid of two forms of psychotherapy, combining psycho-education (which teaches patients and their families about the nature of their illness) with a variety of family therapy. As the name suggests, family therapies are different from other types of therapy because they pay particular attention to family dynamics and relationships, and the part they play in your illness. They are sometimes referred to as 'ecological therapies', because they recognise that individuals and their bipolar cannot be considered separate entities from the family systems that contain them.

FFT therapists work to identify difficulties and conflicts within the family that may contribute to stress for the patient and their close relatives. They then help family members find ways to resolve those problems. 'Expressed emotion' is a term often used in FFT, referring to critical, hostile or over-involved attitudes and behaviours that family members act out with their child, sibling or parent with a psychiatric disorder. For example, the parents of an adolescent son with bipolar may be upset by their child's illness, and so become over-protective or controlling. The son may rebel against this, adding significant stress to an already fraught family set-up. Becoming aware of and bringing under control this expressed emotion is a key part of FFT.

The other part of FFT, psycho-education, helps everyone in the family understand the nature of bipolar disorder, its treatment and the ways family members can best help and support their bipolar relative. This might take the form of lectures or handouts, as well as assistance and training to improve communication and problem-solving skills.

Because bipolar disorder is associated with impulsive and reckless behaviour, as well as suicidal thoughts and impulses, it can be very demanding on every member of a family unit. So family members can easily get burned out from looking after their deeply loved, but challenging bipolar relative. Again, a key part of FFT is supporting the family members acting as carers and a support network. This makes it a powerful tool for fostering and maintaining stability in the family unit.

Counselling

Counselling is the most popular and widely available talking treatment in the UK. The British Association for Counselling and Psychotherapy (BACP) says counselling takes place when: 'A counsellor sees a client in a private and confidential setting to explore a difficulty the client is having, distress they may be experiencing or perhaps their dissatisfaction with life, or loss of direction and purpose.'

The counsellor listens carefully and tries to see your life and the difficulties you are facing from your point of view (being empathic). As well as providing a safe, neutral and non-judgemental space for you to get things off your chest, or explore painful material, good counselling helps you see things from a different perspective (known as 'reframing'). Counselling can also allow you to vent bottled-up feelings like anger, anxiety, grief or embarrassment, which you might not feel comfortable revealing to friends, your partner or even family members.

The type of counselling on offer will vary with the counsellor's theoretical perspective – typically humanistic, psychodynamic, cognitive or behavioural (see www.bacp.co.uk for more information). If you are referred by your GP, you will be offered up to six sessions. If you see a counsellor privately, the work will probably be more open-ended, although any reputable counsellor should offer six sessions first, before you both decide whether you need/want to have more.

A key point here is that some experts feel just sitting and talking about your feelings is not necessarily helpful for bipolar clients. Psycho-education, mood monitoring and learning to control negative or destructive thoughts and behaviours should form part of any effective talking treatment. If you do have counselling, discuss this with your counsellor and make sure they are appropriately trained and able to deal with bipolar disorder's specific issues. For example, if you're having therapy for bipolar depression, there is a chance that the therapy might cause a manic episode. Make sure your therapist is aware of this.

Interpersonal and social rhythm therapy

Interpersonal and social rhythm therapy (IPSRT) is also used to treat bipolar disorder. It's based on the idea that bipolar disorders are essentially body-rhythm disturbances, and that altered body rhythms (such as circadian rhythms, seasonal rhythms and social/work-related rhythms) can lead to disturbances in mood. As we have seen, sleep deprivation is a key trigger for manic episodes, so IPSRT therapists help you set up and stick to healthy sleep routines. As your sleeping routines become stabilised, many problems related to body rhythms tend to go away.

As in CBT, patients working with an IPRST therapist keep a mood chart to track their mood states, daily activities and body rhythms. You will record when you eat, sleep, shop, take your medication, exercise, and so on, as well as noting social interactions like interpersonal conflicts that affect your daily body rhythms and so your mood. This mood chart is an important tool in the therapy sessions, to raise your awareness of the symbiotic relationship between your body rhythms and mood – and for some patients, it's a powerful tool for preventing mood swings.

Getting access to talking therapies

To obtain talking therapies on the NHS, first speak to your GP. If they think it's helpful, they will refer you to a counsellor, family-focused therapist or someone trained in CBT, like a psychologist, nurse, social worker or psychiatrist. Do bear in mind that any type of counselling or psychotherapy is best provided by a skilled, well-trained practitioner – sadly, as the NHS increasingly seeks to cut costs, there is a tendency for people with minimal training to practise CBT, which may not be effective or helpful.

If you are unhappy with your treatment, never be afraid to raise that with your therapist – after all, it's your wellbeing at stake. That should always take precedence over being polite or trying to spare someone's feelings. Also remember that NHS treatment is patchy. Again, sadly, the quality of talking treatments on offer is a 'postcode lottery' in the UK, and will very much depend on where you live.

If you or your family can afford it, you might consider private treatment. The upside to this is that you are likely to get many more sessions than on the NHS – and there is strong evidence to show that, even with time-limited treatments like CBT, longer-term therapy, with follow-up sessions whenever necessary, is far more effective than the six sessions you will be offered in primary care (or 12 in secondary care).

The downside is that, although the government is working to change this, psychotherapy remains an unregulated industry – there are hundreds of counsellors and psychotherapists practising today with dubious training and skill levels. Always find a counsellor or psychotherapist through the main governing bodies: for counsellors, the BACP (www.bacp.co.uk), for psychotherapists the UKCP (www.psychotherapy.org.uk) and for CBT therapists the BABCP (www.babcp.com).

Online/other resources

A vast number of self-help books are available, the best of which you can find in the book list. The Internet is also awash with self-help and psychology websites – many of which are best avoided, because they have very little medical or psychotherapeutic credibility. Most people with bipolar disorder find online forums – where they can share experiences and get support from other people with bipolar – extremely helpful. See the next chapter on self-care, and check out the help list for some of the best.

In England and Wales, you can also access two computer-based programmes provided by the NHS. Fear Fighter is for people with phobias or panic attacks. Beating the Blues is for people with mild to moderate depression. These programmes are not specifically designed for people with bipolar disorder, but you may find them helpful. Before using them, it's a good idea to check with your mental health team.

Summing Up

Research shows that combining talking therapy with medication is the most effective way to treat bipolar disorder. In a major study, when people with bipolar disorder who were experiencing a depressive episode received both intensive psychotherapy and medication, they recovered faster and were less likely to relapse than those who only took medication and had a few sessions educating them about the illness. And the most effective form of talking therapy for bipolar is cognitive behavioural therapy, or CBT. This breaks down overwhelming problems into smaller, more manageable parts. The core principle of CBT is that the way you think affects the way you feel, and therefore the way you act. So learning to identify and prevent negative or self-destructive ways of thinking will help you feel better and prevent unhelpful behaviours.

Learning to manage your moods is another key aspect of CBT. This involves identifying early warning signs of either a manic or depressive episode – once you learn to spot these you can get help to avoid swinging into a full-blown high or low. CBT also helps you understand that mood swings are not inherently bad – 'normalising' short-term ups and downs will help you accept them.

Other talking therapies that can be helpful for bipolar include family focused therapy, counselling and interpersonal and social rhythm therapy. All of these talking treatments are available both privately and through the NHS. But whichever you choose, it's vital that your therapist is skilled, qualified and knowledgeable about treating bipolar. Just talking about your problems is not as helpful as psycho-education or mood management, for example.

You can also get treatment online, especially CBT through the NHS's Fear Fighter and Beating the Blues programmes. Whatever you decide to do, it's always a good idea to discuss it first with your GP or mental health team.

Chapter Eight

How You Can Help Yourself

Managing your bipolar requires a three-pronged approach: medication, talking therapies and self-management. Although they are all important in their own right, in many ways the three areas work together. For example, it's very difficult to find the energy to tackle negative thinking when you're profoundly depressed. So antidepressants can help lift you out of that difficult place enough for talking therapy to be possible, and effective.

Another example is the way 'mood charts' (more on these shortly) can help you understand when your moods go up or down and why. This is invaluable information for your therapist, who can work with you on identifying your triggers as early as possible and understanding how to stop a low mood or hyper frame of mind becoming a full-blown depressive or manic episode.

Mood charts are just one aspect of self-management which, as the name suggests, means you taking responsibility for looking after yourself. As well as recording information about your life and mental state, this involves taking good physical care of yourself, and learning to recognise your triggers – the things that tip you over into a manic or depressive episode. Avoiding these triggers will help you avoid mood swings, and make sure you suffer fewer and less-severe episodes throughout your life.

'Research has shown that learning to self-manage bipolar disorder is an invaluable part of stabilizing the condition.'

MDF: The BiPolar Organisation.

What is self-management?

Self-management is the most powerful tool at your disposal for taking control of your illness. Many people with bipolar disorder feel that things are constantly being done to them: someone may tell you that you need to go into hospital and how long you must stay there; someone else gives you a diagnosis, which you will have for life; and yet another person tells you which medication you should take, exactly which pills you need to swallow and how often. It can feel like the minute you get that diagnosis, your life is no longer in your own hands.

The great thing about self-management is that, once you have learned some basic skills and techniques, you will be in much greater control of both your illness and its treatment – you'll become your own expert (because, after all, who can know more about you than you?). You will come to understand how important it is that you eat well, don't get too stressed, go easy on alcohol and caffeine, and avoid recreational drugs.

You'll learn that the quality of your sleep can tell you when things aren't quite right, and that sleeping well every night is also a key part of staying well. Learning to keep a record of your thoughts, feelings and activities will help you control your mood swings. Regular exercise provides another cheap but effective tool for maintaining your mental equilibrium.

And, crucially, gaining knowledge – from books, the right online resources, experts on bipolar disorder and other people with the illness – will give you back the power you might feel was lost when someone gave you that diagnosis. Taking one of the self-management courses described below will give you practical techniques for improving the quality of your life and, most importantly, will help you realise you are not alone. Millions of people around the world are going through the exact same things that you are.

Writing things down

One of the simplest, but most powerful tools at your disposal is learning to keep a record of key aspects of your life. In *Overcoming Mood Swings: A Self-help Guide Using Cognitive Behavioral Techniques*, Professor Jan Scott (head of Glasgow University's Department of Psychiatry and an expert on bipolar disorder) provides a complete guide to managing your illness. She encourages people with bipolar to make lists, record thoughts, collect information about what they have done, evaluate your their activities and responses to them, and monitor their moods.

Professor Scott argues that writing things down has two important benefits. The first is that, working through her book or with a therapist, you are often asked to do something with the information, like changing a daily activity or tackling unhelpful thoughts. It's much easier to do that if you have a written record of how the techniques applied to you and whether they were helpful.

Second, says Professor Scott: 'Writing it down makes it real. If you write down what you think, it is very powerful. You also gain a little distance from it, and will find working on it a lot easier. Also, many barriers or problems in achieving your goals are far more apparent when you make notes than if you just work through things in your mind.'

A good place to start is with a journal. If you can afford it, it's worth investing in a good-quality notebook, because it's symbolic of the value you place on yourself and your own wellbeing. The way you use that journal is up to you – some people like to write down streams of consciousness, poems, thoughts and dreams. Others are more organised, keeping day-to-day records of their thoughts and feelings, and the events that preceded and followed them. Try and write something every day, if possible – as we will see, that information might prove invaluable in the future.

Learn to self-monitor

One of the ways you can help yourself is by using one of the excellent books aimed at people with mood disorders. See the book list for some suggestions, or try one of the 'Overcoming' series, which offer cognitive-therapy techniques to help manage your mood. Jan Scott's *Overcoming Mood Swings* provides a complete six-month programme you can use as a self-help manual to take control of your moods. It's an excellent book, as is Paul Gilbert's *Overcoming Depression*, which we referred to in chapter 4.

Mood Mapping: Plot Your Way to Emotional Health and Happiness, by Dr Liz Miller, is also strongly recommended. Dr Miller – who has bipolar disorder – offers a straightforward guide to learning how to identify, understand and lift your mood, overcome mood swings and relieve worry and anxiety. Like Jan Scott's book, it offers a complete 'how-to' guide you can work through at your own pace.

Some of the most useful suggestions in *Overcoming Mood Swings* include:

- Becoming an expert on your mood swings, by learning to understand their pattern and the stressors or other factors that cause them.

- Constructing a 'life chart', which shows the number and sequence of each episode, how severe it is and how long it lasts. This is key to understanding the pattern of your mood swings – for example, whether they occur at particular times of year; whether you get low in response to a negative stressor, like pressure at work or breaking up with your boyfriend; or high after a positive stressor, like a wedding or big family party.

- Identifying your 'symptom profile' (see table 1, opposite). This is especially useful for recognising your 'early warning symptoms', so you can take action before becoming depressed or manic.

- Developing a 'risk list'. If you review the events, experiences and behaviours that occurred in the months leading up to a mood disorder, you might be able to identify common themes, and therefore high-risk life events (graduating from college); life situations (these can be positive, such as anniversaries and parties, or negative, such as home/work pressures); and personal actions (consuming alcohol or recreational drugs, or stopping taking your medication).

Need2Know

Symptom Profile

Highs	Depression
Elated and irritable	Very depressed and anxious
My common symptoms are:	
1. Increased energy*	1. Indecisiveness and procrastination*
2. Disinhibited	2. Feeling slowed down
3. Increased spending	3. Loss of appetite/weight*
4. Reduced need for sleep	4. Social withdrawal*
5. Easily distracted	5. Poor sleep with early awakening*
6. Very sociable	6. Lack of energy, feeling lethargic
My less common symptoms are:	
1. Intense optimism	1. Pessimism about the future
2. Increased punning and rhyming	2. Agitation about minor things when I talk
3. Aggressiveness	3. Feelings of guilt and worthlessness
4. Risk-taking	4. Thoughts of death

*Early warning symptoms

Table from *Overcoming Mood Swings* by Jan Scott (Constable & Robinson, London, 2000) by kind permission of the publishers.

Moodscope: a powerful online tool

A new online mood mapping system, Moodscope (www.moodscope.com) provides one of the simplest ways to keep track of your moods. It was developed by former advertising executive Jon Cousins, who has bipolar disorder, because his psychiatrist asked him to keep a diary of his moods but he couldn't find any online resources to help. So he came up with a system of playing cards, based on a reliable mood test (the Positive Affect Negative Affect Schedule, or PANAS). You simply flip the card or spin it round to record a score. For example, for Enthusiastic, you can click on Very little or Not at all, A little, Quite a bit or Extremely. The same goes for Jittery, Anxious, Attentive, Determined, Strong, and so on.

The website automatically calculates an overall mood score between 0 and 100%, then records it on a graph. Record your score every day and you can instantly see the way your mood goes up or down over the week and month. You can also make a note for each point on the graph, so you can look back and see what made you feel up or down that day. Take a look at Jon's chart, below, to see how it looks:

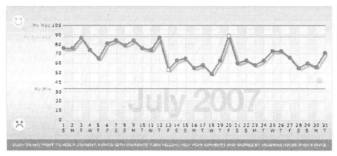

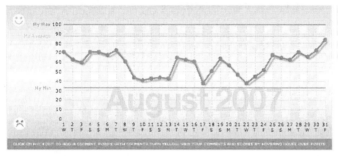

Another crucial element of Moodscope is the 'buddy' system, where you nominate as many buddies as you want. When you record a score they automatically get an email, telling them how you're doing. If your score is lower than usual, they can email or give you a ring to check you're OK.

This is a great way to let your loved ones know how you're doing, and to tell them when you need support without having to pick up the phone. When you're down, it can be especially difficult to reach out, so Moodscope does the job for you.

Jon Cousins explains why he thinks Moodscope is so helpful for managing mood disorders: 'The first thing is that it helps you get down on paper a picture of what's been happening to you. I think when you're about to be or have just been diagnosed, you are going through a really befuddling phase – you don't know what's going on with you, people are asking you all sorts of questions and it's very difficult to be objective about your mental state. So it's amazingly useful to be able to say, "Right, I can show you exactly how I've been."'

If you haven't yet had a diagnosis, but you or your family suspect you may have bipolar disorder, Cousins says you can try Moodscope while you're plucking up the courage to visit your GP. After a month, say, you can print off your mood charts and show him or her exactly how you've been and why you're worried.

And post-diagnosis, when you are receiving treatment, Moodscope is also extremely useful. 'Once you start to go through whatever treatment or interventions are offered to you, it gives you and the clinician the ability to look at what's been happening. So if you're on medication, you can track exactly when your mood changed, or didn't, in response to a particular drug. And the same goes for talking therapies,' says Cousins.

Moodscope is recommended by MDF: The BiPolar Organisation and is being researched by the Institute of Psychiatry. And it offers a really simple and easy way to keep the kind of mood diary suggested by Jan Scott, so it's well worth a try.

Managing your lifestyle

Looking after yourself involves focusing on a few key areas of your lifestyle. This may seem like common sense, but it's easy for us all to neglect certain things we know we should be doing but can't be bothered to. If you have bipolar disorder, not being bothered can cost you dearly, so it really is worth making the effort.

Dr Nick Stafford is a consultant psychiatrist working in the NHS and vice-chair of MDF – the BiPolar Organisation. He also has bipolar disorder, which he manages with a combination of medication and self-care (see his case study following). These are the five key lifestyle areas Dr Stafford recommends you watch out for:

Sleep

Getting good-quality sleep every night is vital if you have bipolar disorder. Of course, this isn't always possible, but try to aim for around eight hours a night. And remember that the quality of your sleep varies according to how late you go to bed, how much alcohol you drink and whether you have caffeine in the evening.

According to Dr Stafford, the quality of your sleep can also be a warning sign of an impending mood swing. 'If your sleep goes off-kilter, it's an early warning sign you must pay attention to. If you're waking up early or not getting enough sleep, you need to do something about that, either by reducing your stress levels or doing exercise, which helps. If necessary, take a sleeping tablet early on – don't wait two weeks to do that,' he says.

Exercise

Research increasingly shows how much exercise can help with both physical and mental health. For example, in a study by researchers from Duke University, in the US, 156 depressed adults aged 50 and over were randomly assigned to four months of thrice-weekly exercise training, medication with an antidepressant, or a combination of the two. After four months, patients in all three groups showed significant and similar reductions in depressive symptoms: 60.4% of patients in the exercise group, 65.5% in the medication-only group and 68.8% in the combined group no longer met the criteria for major depressive disorder.

To combat depression, anxiety or stress, the key is to find something you enjoy and can do regularly. Ideally, you should take up to an hour's aerobic exercise three times a week. Brisk walking, jogging, cycling, swimming and dancing will all have a major impact on your psychological wellbeing. If that's tricky, even a daily 10-15 minute walk will significantly improve your mood.

'Exercise is fantastic – I can't say enough about it,' comments Dr Stafford. 'Regular exercise thwarts early-onset diabetes, weight gain and heart disease – which people with bipolar are at a high risk of developing. It enhances the beneficial effect of your medication and improves your self-esteem and confidence.'

Diet

The key to eating well is to ignore all the faddy diets touted in the media. Make sure you eat a good, well-balanced diet with three meals a day and healthy snacks in between. Follow the same rules that apply to anyone else – avoiding sugary, salty, fatty foods and making sure you get your five-a-day. 'Try to eat a good, well-balanced diet, moderate your calorie intake and eat lots of nuts, fruit and proper vegetables – with, of course, the odd treat,' says Dr Stafford. 'There is a lot of discussion about supplements like omega-3 fish oils but, having looked into it, the evidence is quite thin on the ground.'

Drugs

All drugs, whether legal or illegal, have a powerful effect on our mood. If your mood is changeable, you need to be very careful about the drugs you introduce into your system. Even caffeine, found in tea, coffee and many fizzy drinks, will give you an initial energy boost followed by a crash, and can have a major impact on your sleep. Many people with mood disorders use alcohol to suppress painful emotions or give them more confidence in social situations, ignoring the fact that alcohol is a depressant. That's one of the reasons you feel so awful with a hangover.

Recreational drug use is also very common in people with a mental health problem. But drugs like cannabis, ecstasy, cocaine and heroin have a powerful effect on your mood. In fact, depressive symptoms can develop as a direct result of taking these drugs, or as part of the withdrawal symptoms when drug-taking stops.

It's ironic that these drugs affect the chemicals in our brain which make us feel good – neurotransmitters like dopamine, serotonin and noradrenaline. Cocaine, for example, boosts the amount of dopamine in your brain, making you feel confident and full of self-belief. But the day-after comedown can be brutal, because your brain is now low on dopamine, leading to depression, paranoia and even suicidal feelings.

Ideally, of course, you should avoid recreational drugs completely and take both caffeine and alcohol in moderation. If you are struggling with alcohol or drug dependence or addiction, speak to your GP, mental health professional or visit a website like Frank (www.talktofrank.com), which is packed with information and offers free advice by email, text or phone.

Stress

Minimising daily stress is a crucial part of managing your illness. This can be impossible in some jobs, like high-pressure sales or deadline-driven roles, so after receiving a diagnosis many people opt for less pressurised careers. This can be a tough decision to make, but ultimately your wellbeing is far more important than how much money you make or the type of car you drive.

'I have learnt to my cost that if you don't manage your stress you're going to be in trouble,' says Dr Stafford. 'You have to know your own limits and not take too much on. So in my job, I'm surrounded by people I want to do too much for: patients, colleagues, and so on. I have to continually check that, because if I'm misguided by a sense of devotion to my profession, it will only make me ill.'

Stress will affect your ability to sleep, your levels of anger and irritation, your confidence, happiness and general sense of wellbeing. And consistently high levels of stress, or a single stressful event like a divorce, can cause a manic or depressive episode. Two excellent books on stress are *How to Deal With Stress*, by Stephen Palmer and Cary Cooper; and *Beating Stress, Anxiety and Depression*, by Professor Jane Plant and Janet Stephenson.

Self-management courses

There are a number of self-management courses available for people with bipolar, their friends, families and carers. These courses can be invaluable, both in terms of what they teach you and as a place to meet other people who are going through exactly the same thing as you. It's very easy to become isolated when you have an illness like bipolar disorder, so spending time in a group with other bipolar sufferers can be a great source of support, and potentially friendship.

MDF: The BiPolar Organisation has run its free self-management training course for many years now. Each course has six modules, with 14 participants and two facilitators (both of whom have bipolar disorder). Over the six sessions, you will learn: to identify your triggers and warning signs; coping strategies and self-medication; support networks and action plans; strategies for maintaining a healthy lifestyle and drawing up an advance directive (a legal document that says what kind of treatment you want to receive if you are too ill to make decisions for yourself); and which complementary therapies can help.

MDF also offers STEADY, a self-management programme for people aged 18-25 with bipolar disorder. It is also developing a new web-based psycho-educational programme in-conjunction with the Mood Disorders Research Group at Cardiff University. Called 'Beating Bipolar', it's made up of eight 20-minute interactive modules, available online over a four-month period. MDF hopes the interactive version will be available this year, but selected resources are available now at www.mdf.org.uk

Another excellent programme, the 'New Beginnings' Mental Health Course, is available through the Expert Patients Programme Community Interest Company (EPP CIC). This free self-management course consists of seven consecutive weekly sessions, and is aimed at people living with, or in recovery from a mental health problem. Like the MDF course, New Beginnings is run by trained facilitators who also have bipolar disorder. Topics covered include problem-solving and goal-setting; confidence-building; anxiety and depression management; triggers and relapse symptom awareness; positive thinking; relaxation techniques; healthy lifestyle; communicating with family, friends and professionals; and planning for the future.

Jim Phillips, head of policy at EPP CIC, says the course can produce major and long-lasting effects. 'Typically, after the course we see people with increased confidence going into higher education or back to work, developing new social networks and reconnecting with their family. It can also mean the difference between staying in a marriage or job or not, so it can have a major influence on people's lives.'

Phillips says one of the biggest benefits for people with bipolar disorder is being somewhere they feel understood. 'You don't have to explain yourself, you just know the other people understand exactly what you're talking about,' he says. 'You don't have to go into some long story. People really know what you're going through, as opposed to a health professional who nods sympathetically but has never been through it themselves.'

For more information or to find a course in your area, talk to your GP or visit www.expertpatients.co.uk

Dr Nick Stafford is a consultant psychiatrist who has bipolar disorder – here he explains how he manages his illness with a combination of medication and self-care

'Looking back, I think I've probably had this illness since my teens, but I had my first episode at the age of 30, back in 1997. That was a full-blown manic episode which required hospitalisation for about a week. I got a formal diagnosis and started the long journey most people go on. I was put on medication, which was adjusted until the initial episode subsided.

'Since then I've had the occasional episode every few years and needed either rest or treatment to get over that. But I've been very lucky because, apart from taking time off when I need to, I've been working ever since.

'I have Bipolar I, so I had that manic episode and a couple of serious depressions. But I'm usually either OK or grumble along with a bit of irritability, which needs anything from exercise or rest to changing my meds a bit. And I've always taken medication, every day since 1997 – I currently take sodium valproate, lithium carbonate and folate, which is something I've added myself.

'I know from experience, both personally and having treated thousands of people with this illness, that without medication you're doing yourself a massive disservice. It's a very serious biological illness and requires serious treatment – that's just common sense.

'But self-care is also hugely important. For myself, I've always struggled with managing my stress. I do a stressful job and I'm a father of two, as well as working with MDF and having other things going on. But I've learned to my cost that if you don't manage your stress you are in trouble. You have to know your own limits and not take too much on.

'Good-quality sleep is vital and, over the last few years, I've also taken a good look at my diet and exercise. That just means having a well-balanced diet and avoiding all the refined stuff, especially sugary things. I've lost three stone and my mood seems much better for it.

'Finally, I only drink alcohol in moderation. A couple of units a night is fine, but because you enjoy it and never to control your mood or help you sleep. And exercise is fantastic – it's helped me lose all that weight and makes a massive difference to my mood and general wellbeing.'

Summing Up

Self-management is a vital part of keeping your bipolar in check. Combined with medication and talking therapies, it's a powerful tool that lets you take control of your illness, rather than letting it control you. The first part of self-management is increasing your knowledge, with books like this one and those in the book list, charities like MDF: The BiPolar Organisation; online resources, like the Royal College of Psychiatrists' website; and other people with bipolar. Knowledge, as they say, is power.

The next step is learning to monitor your thoughts, activities and moods, by writing them down in a journal. This information will prove invaluable when it comes to working with a therapist, or to help your psychiatrist understand how you react to different kinds of medication. Crucially, you need to become an expert in your own moods and what triggers them. One of the best ways to do this is with a mood chart – visit Moodscope, a free online resource that helps you track your day-to-day moods, to find out more.

You also need to manage your lifestyle, focusing on the five key areas of sleep, exercise, diet, drugs (both legal and recreational) and stress. Learning to live a healthy, reasonably stress-free life will have a profound effect on your bipolar. It will increase the effectiveness of your medication, stop you from suffering severe mood swings and can add up to 10 years to your life.

Finally, you can go on a self-management course. These typically last for six or seven weeks, are free, and available through MDF or Expert Patients (see the help list for details). These courses not only teach you about things like your triggers and warning signs, coping strategies and self-medication, but are a great place to find support from people who understand exactly what you're going through.

Chapter Nine

How You Can Help a Friend or Relative with Bipolar Disorder

When someone develops a mental illness like bipolar disorder, the impact can be profound for everyone who knows and loves them. Work colleagues, friends, family members, partner, children . . . all will be affected in some way. If someone you know and love has been diagnosed with bipolar, one of the things you will need to do is get support for yourself, because the practical and emotional load can be a heavy one.

But you also have a key role to play in supporting your friend or loved one by helping them get the best possible treatment, providing practical help with everything from housework to getting to their appointments, and offering much-needed emotional support when they are going through a rough time. As we have seen earlier in the book, one of the greatest difficulties facing people with bipolar disorder is isolation, so making sure they have a strong, supportive network in place is crucial – and could, quite literally, be life-saving.

> 'This illness can stop people in their tracks, but once they've negotiated all the initial hurdles they can have a quieter, simpler, less stressful but still good-quality life.'
>
> Daisy Jellicoe, membership officer, MDF: The BiPolar Organisation.

How you can help

One of the most important things you can do for your friend or relative is to get involved in their treatment. Sadly, NHS mental health services are patchy and some GPs are much more compassionate and dedicated than others. As soon as someone receives a diagnosis they will be confronted with a bewildering range of treatment options, including different medications and talking therapies. If this diagnosis comes after their first manic episode, as it often does, they are likely to need all the help they can get – especially if they have been sectioned under the Mental Health Act.

Daisy Jellicoe, who has bipolar disorder and is membership services officer for MDF – The BiPolar Organisation, says friends and families need to be extremely proactive in their dealings with doctors. 'It's critical to find a good GP and psychiatrist. And it's very important for the person with bipolar to be quite assertive when dealing with doctors, backed up by their family. You both need to establish a good relationship with your doctor and psychiatrist, because the drugs can be so hard on your system. You will have to try a number of different drugs and there may be unpleasant side effects, so you need to have faith in your psychiatrist. If you don't have one you like, find another one.'

The NICE guidelines for the treatment of bipolar disorder (see book list) state that if someone in your family has bipolar, healthcare professionals should give you information about the illness and treatments that can help. They should also be available in times of crisis. Doctors should consider their needs, especially if they are under 18, they should be offered a regular assessment of their circumstances and they may be offered treatment and support.

NICE also suggests asking the doctor the following questions:

- What can we do to help someone with bipolar disorder?

- Is there anywhere we can get extra support?

- We feel stressed and are not sleeping well. Can you give me advice on how we can cope with this?

- Are there any ways we can reduce stress while trying to live a normal life?

- How can we help our children cope with living with someone with bipolar disorder?

- Can our child's school get help and advice on dealing with the effects of bipolar disorder?

It's also a good idea to request double appointments with the GP so you have a bit more time to talk about their symptoms and explore options for treatment. And try to write a list of questions, like the ones above, before your appointment. Otherwise it's easy to forget what you wanted to ask – and you may not get another chance for months.

Practical support

The best support you can give a friend or relative with bipolar is to give them your love, strength and encouragement, no matter what. That alone will make a huge difference and will help them avoid manic or depressive episodes, and affect both how long the episodes last and how severe they are. But there is a great deal you can do practically, too.

The NICE guidelines also say that friends and family can:

▒ Help the person recognise the onset of symptoms.

▒ Support them through crises.

▒ Provide healthcare professionals with information about symptoms and behaviour. This will help doctors understand how well medications are working, and is very important for talking treatments like cognitive behavioural therapy.

On a day-to-day level, there's all sorts of practical help you can offer, including:

▒ Picking up prescriptions and medication.

▒ Keeping their diary up to date so they don't miss appointments.

▒ Driving them to appointments.

▒ Encouraging them to see their GP or community mental health team and going with them to support groups.

▒ Doing their shopping, domestic chores and cooking favourite meals.

▒ Sorting out bills and household admin.

It's also a good idea to plan ahead for a possible relapse, by making a list of warning signs; keeping a list of useful numbers for an emergency, like the community mental health team, GP and psychiatrist; and discussing what action they need to take in different scenarios.

Emotional and psychological support

There are likely to be key times when someone needs more support: before they get a diagnosis and can receive treatment, when they may be very ill; when they are starting to take medication and will probably experience some unpleasant and potentially frightening side effects; when they are going through a manic or depressive episode; and after an episode, when they are trying to get back on their feet.

The most important thing you can do is to be kind, supportive, non-judgemental and consistent – they need to know they can rely on you, even when their behaviour may be challenging. Remember that this behaviour is strongly influenced by chemical imbalances in their brain. It's not their fault and they certainly wouldn't choose to have this illness or behave in ways that cause themselves and others problems.

You will also need to invest time and energy in your relationship with them, so you'll need some specific skills and tools do so. In *Overcoming Mood Swings: A Self-help Guide Using Cognitive Behavioral Techniques* (see book list), Jan Scott says communication is vital for maintaining healthy relationships. Here's an abbreviated version of her advice for tackling interpersonal problems – which applies equally to people with bipolar disorder and those trying to support them:

- Take your time to think about what you need to say and what issue you're trying to get across.

- Be clear about the problem, but make sure you own it. Avoid placing all the responsibility on the other person, which may lead to them becoming defensive or angry.

- Avoid sweeping statements and words like 'always' or 'never'.

- Try to develop a shared view of the problem – if you can't agree about that, you will never agree on the solution.

- Be a good listener and don't interrupt.

- If the conversation is getting heated, take some time out. In general, try to stay calm – when angry, we often say and do things we regret.

If anger is a problem for you or the person with bipolar disorder, you may need to consider an anger management course. Ask your GP for local resources or visit the British Association of Anger Management's (BAAM) website: www. angermanage.co.uk – it offers a wide range of resources. You may also want to read *Anger Management – The Essential Guide*, by Wendy Sloane (Need-2-Know) or *Beating Anger: The 8-point Plan for Coping With Rage*, by Mike Fisher, BAAM's founder.

Case study

Sonia McDuff, 33, from Folkestone, was diagnosed with bipolar disorder when she was 29

'I was very unwell with depression in my early twenties, but I seemed to get through that. My bipolarity didn't come out till 2006, after a combination of positive and negative stressful life events led to a manic episode. It took a while to get diagnosed and I was very unwell for a long time. I did all the typical manic stuff of putting horrendous offers in on houses, boats and cars, got stranded in New York and hitch-hiked round Ireland before I eventually crash-landed at my mum's.

'I didn't know where I was and had no clue that it might have been bipolar disorder. But all the people closest to me knew before I did that something was wrong. And my mum realised when we were watching Stephen Fry's documentary – she stared at me throughout the programme, because she recognised a lot of the symptoms.

'I also realised that a lot of it rang true, but I wasn't sure what to do next. I phoned a friend, who encouraged me to see my doctor. I did, then saw a psychologist and eventually, after a series of psychiatric appointments, I was diagnosed as bipolar.

'In the short term that was a relief, but in the long term it's been hard to accept. When you have a normal livelihood – I was a freelance photographer – and lifestyle, it's really hard to accept that you have this label attached to you for life. After I got my diagnosis I was leading a completely different life, living with my mum and working in a pub. That was good for a short time, because I made new friends and needed some stability. But it was a totally different lifestyle than before I got ill.

'And that's difficult for those around you too. If you know a person when they are well – and I was well for a long time – it's hard for them to accept the way you are now. I think my mum's finding it incredibly challenging, because the person she knew isn't there anymore. She finds that really hard and there doesn't seem to be much support for carers like her.

'My social worker recommended the New Beginnings self-management course and I've found it really helpful. I am now living in my own property and I work for myself again, although in a different capacity, by running a community arts project, among other things. I also want to study art psychotherapy, as my illness has given me a valuable insight into mental health needs in terms of the wider community.'

Looking after yourself

Studies have shown that people with bipolar do best in happy, stable families. So looking after your own needs will not only help you stay sane and keep your energy levels up when times are hard, but will have a direct impact on the health and relapse rate of your bipolar friend or family member. After they get a diagnosis, it's also a good idea to be realistic and expect some challenging times ahead.

Daisy Jellicoe confirms that bipolar can be tough for everyone concerned: 'It can be completely devastating for the family. People's personalities change so much – having been happy-go-lucky and carefree, suddenly they can't get out of bed, or they're irritable, angry and frustrated. They may even lash out at those around them, because they're just so desperate.'

She adds that this can be especially difficult when people are going through a low or high phase: 'Both extremes are awful. Depression sucks away your energy and everything looks very bleak. They may have suicidal thoughts, which are terrible for parents to hear. And at the other end they might be paranoid and terrified of all sorts of things, which is also really tough to deal with.'

If you are having a hard time supporting someone with bipolar, talk to your GP. You may need counselling or some other support. MDF – the BiPolar Organisation runs self-help groups for people with bipolar and their friends/families. These can be a great source of help and support. And make sure you take the time to nourish yourself: do things you enjoy, spend time with friends, get regular exercise – you need to do all the things recommended in chapter 8 to keep yourself healthy and well.

If your child or partner becomes ill, it's important that you remember it's not your fault. Bipolar disorder is caused by a combination of genetic and environmental factors, and usually triggered by a stressful life event – all of which may have nothing to do with you. As a parent, it's natural to worry about your children and want to protect and do the best for them. But feeling guilty or blaming yourself won't help them or you. Instead, focus on being there for them, providing love, support and encouragement as they begin the long journey towards managing their illness and living the best life that they can.

And Daisy Jellicoe says that, however hard things seem at first, it should get easier with time: 'There is light at the end of the tunnel. This illness can stop people in their tracks, but once they've negotiated all the initial hurdles they can have a quieter, simpler, less stressful but still good-quality life. There is hope, however hard it seems.'

Summing Up

If a friend or relative has bipolar disorder, you have a crucial role to play. They will need your help in a number of ways from the moment they receive a diagnosis – and probably before that, when they are likely to have been very ill. One of the biggest areas you can help with is their treatment, making sure they have a good relationship with their GP and psychiatrist and that they are getting the best possible care.

When they start taking medication, they may well experience unpleasant and potentially frightening side effects, so having the support of a friend or loved one will be vital. They may also need practical support, like help with their shopping or being driven to appointments, and emotional support, especially when they are going through a depressive or manic episode and immediately afterwards.

This relationship may well be challenging for you both, so it's worth learning some specific communication skills to help keep it on track. And it's important that you look after yourself, by asking your GP for help if you are unable to cope or going to a self-help group where you can meet other carers who understand what you're going through. Make sure you take good care of your physical and mental health too.

Let's end on a positive note: although bipolar disorder can be an extremely challenging illness, both for the person with bipolar and those around them, the treatment available has come on in leaps and bounds in recent years. Medication like lithium, antipsychotics and antidepressants can be life-changing for many people with bipolar. Talking treatments like cognitive behavioural therapy and self-management strategies enable people with bipolar to take control of their illness and, in many cases, lead productive, fulfilling lives.

Glossary of Terms

Acute
A disease with a rapid onset and short course (as opposed to chronic).

Antidepressant
A drug prescribed to relieve the symptoms of depression.

Antipsychotic
A drug prescribed to alleviate psychosis, mania and hypomania.

Bipolar disorder
A mental illness characterised by mood swings.

CAMHS (child and adolescent mental health)
Health services for children and young people under the age of 18.

Care plan
A series of action points chosen and written down by the person with bipolar disorder and their support team, which plan for their future care.

Carer
A person who cares for a sick or elderly person.

CBT (cognitive behavioural therapy)
A talking therapy that aims to modify the unhelpful thoughts and beliefs which cause dysfunctional emotions and behaviours.

Chronic
A persistent and lasting disease or medical condition (as opposed to acute).

Circadian clock
Another name for the body clock that controls our sleep-wake cycle, eating habits, body temperature and hormone secretion.

Community Mental Health Team (CMHT)
Commonly includes a psychiatrist, community psychiatric nurse (CPN), social worker, occupational therapist (OT), clinical psychologist and pharmacist.

Counselling

A form of talking therapy that provides a safe, confidential space for clients to discuss difficulties they may be having or distress they may be experiencing.

CPA (Care Programme Approach)

A care plan designed for someone who has been in hospital. Helps ease their transition back to life outside the hospital.

CPN (Community Psychiatric Nurse)

Nurses who support those with mental illnesses when they are not in hospital.

Crisis Resolution Team (CRT)

Provides 24-hour support for anyone experiencing a mental health crisis.

Cyclothymia

When manic or depressive symptoms last for two years or more, but are not serious enough for a diagnosis of bipolar disorder.

Depression

A persistent low mood, loss of energy and pleasure in previously enjoyable activities.

Diagnostic and Statistical Manual of Mental Disorders (DSM IV)

The fourth edition of a manual published by the American Psychiatric Association. Used in both the UK and US for categorising and diagnosing mental health problems.

Dopamine

A neurotransmitter that transmits signals between nerve cells and is part of the 'reward system', inducing pleasurable sensations in the brain.

Dual diagnosis

When a diagnosis such as bipolar disorder is accompanied by another clinical condition, such as drug addiction.

Family-focused therapy (FFT)

A form of talking treatment which combines psycho-education (teaching patients and their families about the nature of their illness) with a variety of family therapy.

GP (general practitioner)

A family doctor who treats people in the community.

Grandiosity
Delusions of power or superiority.

Hallucination
Seeing, smelling or hearing an object, person or experience that is not actually present.

Holding power
A legal process that allows a doctor to detain and assess a patient in hospital for 72 hours while they decide whether an application for a section needs to be made. A psychiatric nurse can exercise a holding power for up to six hours until a doctor can begin the assessment.

Holistic
Treating all aspects of the person, including their mind, emotions and body, not just the symptoms of their illness.

Hypomania
A persistent mild elevation of mood.

Hypothyroidism
A condition in which the thyroid gland doesn't produce enough of the hormone thyroxine.

Informal patient
Anyone who admits themselves to a psychiatric hospital voluntarily.

Insomnia
Persistent problems with sleep.

Interpersonal and social rhythm therapy
A form of talking therapy based on the idea that bipolar disorders are essentially body-rhythm disturbances.

Lithium
A medicine used to treat mood disorders such as severe depression or bipolar disorder.

Mania
An unnaturally high, euphoric mood.

Manic depression
The former name of bipolar disorder.

Mixed state
When symptoms of mania and depression occur at the same time.

Mood disorder
A mental illness, such as bipolar disorder, in which a disturbance with the person's mood is the main underlying feature.

Nearest relative
A patient's closest family member, who has certain rights.

Neurotransmitters
Chemicals that relay nerve impulses between brain and body.

NICE (National Institute for Clinical Excellence)
An independent organisation responsible for providing national guidance on the promotion of good health and the prevention/treatment of ill health in the UK.

Occupational therapy
The assessment and treatment of physical and psychiatric conditions using specific activities to improve all aspects of daily life.

OTC (over the counter)
Medicines that can be bought at any pharmacy without a prescription.

Paranoia
Delusional thinking in which someone feels persecuted.

Personality disorder
A mental illness characterised by a severe disturbance of someone's character, logic and behaviour.

Psychiatrist
A doctor specialising in mental illness.

Psycho-education
Teaches patients and their families about the nature of their illness.

Psychologist
A person qualified to study the human mind and treat mental illness.

Psychosis
A loss of contact with external reality.

Puerperal psychosis
A condition where symptoms of confusion, hallucinations and a loss of reality happen suddenly, often after childbirth.

Rapid cycling
Experiencing more than four mood swings in one year.

RORB gene
One of the 'clock genes' that controls our circadian clock. Scientists believe that an alteration in this gene is associated with bipolar disorder.

Schizoaffective disorder
A diagnosis that is used when someone does not have either typical schizophrenia or a typical mood disorder.

Schizophrenia
A mental illness involving psychological symptoms such as hallucinations, delusions and changes in behaviour.

Seasonal affective disorder (SAD)
A type of seasonal depression thought to be caused by a lack of sunlight in the winter months.

Section
Compulsory admittance to a psychiatric hospital or ward.

Serotonin
A neurotransmitter known as the brain's 'happy chemical'.

SNRIs (serotonin-norepinephrine reuptake inhibitors)
A class of antidepressant including Effexor and Cymbalta.

SSRIs (selective serotonin reuptake inhibitors)
A class of antidepressant including Prozac and Seroxat.

Talking therapy
Treating mental health problems using a therapy like counselling or CBT, either instead of or in-conjunction with medication.

Tricyclic
An older class of antidepressant largely replaced by SNRIs and SSRIs.

Ultra rapid cycling

When someone experiences monthly, weekly or even daily mood swings.

Unipolar

Describes depression where only low mood is experienced.

Withdrawal symptoms

The unpleasant physical and emotional reaction that occurs when an addictive substance is no longer taken.

Help list

Resources

Alcoholics Anonymous

Tel: 0845 769 7555 (helpline)
www.alcoholics-anonymous.org.uk
An informal society of millions of recovered alcoholics worldwide who follow a 12-step programme to become sober and remain so. AA meetings are available across the UK.

Bipolar4all

www.bipolar4all.co.uk
Describes itself as 'A safe haven for anyone touched by bipolar disorder'. Provides information on bipolar disorder, treatments and support – including the busy Bipolar4all forum.

British Association for Anger Management (BAAM)

Tel: 0845 1300 286
www.angermanage.co.uk
BAAM is the UK's leading organisation for all aspects of anger and conflict management. It runs evening and weekend courses, and has a wide range of resources and information on its website.

British Association for Behavioural and Cognitive Psychotherapies (BABCP)

Victoria Buildings, 9-13 Silver Street, Bury BL9 0EU
Tel: 0161 797 2670
www.babcp.com

BABCP is the leading organisation for cognitive behavioural therapy (CBT) in the UK and can help people find therapists in their local area.

British Association for Counselling and Psychotherapy (BACP)

BACP House, 15 St John's Business Park, Lutterworth LE17 4HB
Tel: 01455 883 316
bacp@bacp.co.uk
www.bacp.co.uk
The umbrella organisation for counselling in the UK. It should be your first port of call if you are looking to see a counsellor privately.

Centre for Stress Management

PO Box 26583, London SE3 7EZ
Tel: 020 7318 4448
www.managingstress.com
Runs cognitive-behavioural training programmes and offers executive, business, performance, stress and life coaching.

Depression Alliance

Depression Alliance, 20 Great Dover Street, London SE1 4LX
Tel: 0845 123 23 20
information@depressionalliance.org
www.depressionalliance.org
Working to relieve and prevent depression by providing information and support services to those who are affected by it via publications, supporter services and a network of self-help groups for people affected by depression.

eHealth Forum

http://ehealthforum.com/health/bipolar_disorder.html
Health community featuring member and doctor discussions ranging from a specific symptom to related conditions, treatment options, medication, side effects, diet and emotional issues surrounding bipolar disorder.

Institute for Complementary and Natural Medicine (ICNM)

Can-Mezzanine, 32-36 Loman Street, London SE1 0EH

Tel: 020 7922 7980

www.i-c-m.org.uk

Providing information on a wide range of complementary therapies and access to a register of qualified complementary therapists across the UK.

Institute of Family Therapy

24-32 Stephenson Way, London NW1 2HX

Tel: 020 7391 9150

www.instituteoffamilytherapy.org.uk

Providing counselling, therapy and mediation for families needing help.

MDF: the BiPolar Organisation

Castle Works, 21 St George's Road, London SE1 6ES

Tel: 020 7793 2600 (to become a member)

mdf@mdf.org.uk

www.mdf.org.uk

National user-led organisation and registered charity for people whose lives are affected by bipolar disorder. It aims to enable people affected by bipolar disorder to take control of their lives through a wide range of services, advice and support.

MIND

15-19 Broadway, Stratford, London E15 4BQ

Tel: 0845 766 0163 (helpline, Monday to Friday, 9am-5pm)

www.mind.org.uk

Providing information and advice to help people take control of their mental health.

Moodscope

www.moodscope.com

Free online mood-monitoring system, allowing you to keep a daily mood score and then record that on a chart plotting your moods over weeks and months. Invaluable tool for keeping track of your moods, then using that information for self-care and with your therapist and/or psychiatrist.

National Debtline

Tel: 0808 808 4000 (helpline, Monday to Friday 9am-9pm and Saturday 9.30am-1pm)
www.nationaldebtline.co.uk
Helpline providing free, confidential and independent advice on dealing with debt problems. Their advice is tailored to people living in different parts of the UK, because the law concerning debt is different in England, Wales and Scotland.

NHS Direct

Tel: 0845 4647 (helpline, Monday to Sunday, 24 hours)
www.nhsdirect.nhs.uk
Providing expert health advice, information and reassurance through a helpline and website.

Pendulum

www.pendulum.org
Extensive online resource on every aspect of bipolar disorder.

Relate

Premier House, Carolina Court, Lakeside, Doncaster DN4 5RA
Tel: 0300 100 1234
www.relate.org.uk
Charity offering advice, support, relationship counselling, sex therapy, workshops, mediation, consultations and support. You can either meet with a counsellor face to face, by phone or through their website.

Rethink

89 Albert Embankment, London SE1 7TP
Tel: 0845 456 0455 (helpline)
www.rethink.org
The leading national mental health membership charity working to help everyone affected by severe mental illness recover a better quality of life.

Royal College of Psychiatrists

17 Belgrave Square, London SW1X 8PG
Tel: 020 7235 2351
www.rpsych.ac.uk
The professional and educational body for psychiatrists in the United Kingdom and the Republic of Ireland. Its website provides an extensive resource on every aspect of mental health and wellbeing.

Samaritans

Chris, PO Box 9090, Stirling, FK8 2SA
Tel: 08457 90 90 90 (helpline, Monday to Sunday, 24-hour)
Tel: 1850 60 90 90 (helpline, Monday to Sunday, 24-hour, Republic of Ireland)
jo@samaritans.org
www.samaritans.org
Samaritans provides confidential, non-judgemental emotional support 24 hours a day for people who are experiencing feelings of distress or despair, including those which could lead to suicide.

SANE

1st Floor, Cityside House, 40 Adler Street, London E1 1EE
Tel: 0845 767 8000 (helpline, Monday to Sunday, 6pm-11pm)
sanemail@sane.org.uk
www.sane.org.uk
SANE is most famous for its national telephone line, which helps over 2,000 men, women and children every month who are affected by mental health issues.

Stand to Reason

info@standtoreason.org.uk
www.standtoreason.org.uk
Service user-led organisation that intends to work with and for people with mental ill health in the way that Stonewall has for gay people: raising the profile of mental illness, fighting prejudice, establishing rights and achieving equality.

Thyromind

www.thyromind.info
Information about thyroid disorders and the importance of thyroid function tests as part of the assessment of a mental health problem.

UK Narcotics Anonymous

Tel: 0300 999 1212 (helpline)
www.ukna.org
An informal society of millions of recovered drug addicts worldwide who follow a 12-step programme to free themselves from addiction. NA meetings are available across the UK.

United Kingdom Council for Psychotherapy (UKCP)

2nd Floor, Edward House, 2 Wakeley Street, London EC1V 7LT
Tel: 020 7014 9955
info@ukcp.org.uk
www.psychotherapy.org.uk
Umbrella organisation for psychotherapy in the UK. It should be your first port of call if you are looking to see a psychotherapist privately.

Book List

Mike Fisher, *Beating Anger: The Eight-Point Plan for Coping With Rage*, Random House, London, 2005

Paul Gilbert, *Overcoming Depression: A Self-Help Guide Using Cognitive Behavioral Techniques*, Constable & Robinson, London, 1997

Dr Liz Miller, *Mood Mapping: Plot Your Way to Emotional Health and Happiness*, Pan Macmillan, London, 2009

Sarah Owen and Amanda Saunders, *Bipolar Disorder: The Ultimate Guide*, Oneworld, Oxford, 2008

Jane Plant and Janet Stephenson, *Beating Stress, Anxiety and Depression: Groundbreaking Ways to Help You Feel Better*, Piatkus, London, 2008

Dorothy Rowe, *Depression: The Way Out of Your Prison*, Routledge, New York, 1983

Robert M Sapolsky, *Why Zebras Don't Get Ulcers: The Acclaimed Guide to Stress, Stress-Related Diseases and Coping*, Holt Paperbacks, New York, 2004

Jan Scott, *Overcoming Mood Swings: A Self-Help Guide Using Cognitive Behavioral Techniques*, Constable & Robinson, London, 2001

Jeremy Thomas and Dr Tony Hughes, *The A-Z Guide to Good Mental Health: You Don't Need to be Famous to Have Manic Depression*, Penguin, London, 2008

Reports, studies and leaflets

Bipolar Disorder (Manic Depression) leaflet, Royal College of Psychiatrists (available from www.rcpsych.ac.uk)

Cognitive Behavioural Therapy (CBT) leaflet, Royal College of Psychiatrists (available from www.rcpsych.ac.uk)

David Miklowitz, Psychosocial Treatments for Bipolar Depression, University of Colorado, published in the April 2007 issue of the journal Archives of General Psychiatry

MIND, In the Red: Debt and Mental Health, 2008

National Institute for Health and Clinical Excellence (NICE) (2005) CG38. Bipolar disorder: the management of bipolar disorder in adults, children and adolescents, in primary and secondary care.

Need - 2 - Know

Available Titles Include ...

Allergies A Parent's Guide
ISBN 978-1-86144-064-8 £8.99

Autism A Parent's Guide
ISBN 978-1-86144-069-3 £8.99

Blood Pressure The Essential Guide
ISBN 978-1-86144-067-9 £8.99

Dyslexia and Other Learning Difficulties
A Parent's Guide ISBN 978-1-86144-042-6 £8.99

Bullying A Parent's Guide
ISBN 978-1-86144-044-0 £8.99

Epilepsy The Essential Guide
ISBN 978-1-86144-063-1 £8.99

Your First Pregnancy The Essential Guide
ISBN 978-1-86144-066-2 £8.99

Gap Years The Essential Guide
ISBN 978-1-86144-079-2 £8.99

Secondary School A Parent's Guide
ISBN 978-1-86144-093-8 £9.99

Primary School A Parent's Guide
ISBN 978-1-86144-088-4 £9.99

Applying to University The Essential Guide
ISBN 978-1-86144-052-5 £8.99

ADHD The Essential Guide
ISBN 978-1-86144-060-0 £8.99

Student Cookbook – Healthy Eating The Essential Guid
ISBN 978-1-86144-069-3 £8.99

Multiple Sclerosis The Essential Guide
ISBN 978-1-86144-086-0 £8.99

Coeliac Disease The Essential Guide
ISBN 978-1-86144-087-7 £9.99

Special Educational Needs A Parent's Guide
ISBN 978-1-86144-116-4 £9.99

The Pill An Essential Guide
ISBN 978-1-86144-058-7 £8.99

University A Survival Guide
ISBN 978-1-86144-072-3 £8.99

View the full range at **www.need2knowbooks.co.uk**.
To order our titles call **01733 898103**, email **sales@
n2kbooks.com** or visit the website. Selected ebooks
available online.

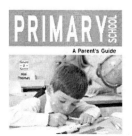

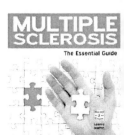

Need - 2 - Know, Remus House, Coltsfoot Drive, Peterborough, PE2 9BF